INSIGHT POCKET GUIDES

CHICAGO

APA PUBLICATIONS
Part of the Langenscheidt Publishing Group

L

Welcome!

First-time visitors often find that Chicago exceeds its reputation. From its vibrant lakefront where city-dwellers flock in the summer months, to the hospitable neighborhoods where they live, you'll find museums, theaters, shopping, restaurants, art galleries, festivals, unique architecture and great sports events. What Chicagoans don't know about having fun isn't worth knowing, and as a consequence there's always something going on.

Although Chicago is dubbed the City of Big Shoulders or the Windy City, it's really the people who make it what it is. Chicagoans are surprisingly friendly for a big city, and show their pride in their home town by readily offering advice on what to see and do. So if you're unsure of something, don't waste valuable vacation time wondering – just ask. If you feel you'll barely arrive before it's time to leave, our Insight correspondent has planned three full-day tours covering Chicago's highlights. Able to stretch your stay? You'll be spoiled for choice with our 11 Pick & Mix options. The back of the book contains sections on shopping, eating out and nightlife as well as loads of practical tips.

Pam Hardy previously contributed to *Insight Guide: Chicago*. A native Chicagoan, she has lived in several suburbs as well as the city itself, and now shares a home in one of the town's historical neighborhoods with her husband and two sons. Pam knows her favorite city inside out, and here she looks forward to helping you discover everything there is to know about when to come, what to do, where to stay and how to eat well – in short, how to have the best possible time here once you've arrived. Welcome to Chicago.

CONTENTS

History & Culture

Who discovered the marshland that became Chicago and why did they choose to settle here? What were the circumstances that brought Chicago's architecture under the world's spotlight? And what did Al Capone have to do with Chicago politics? Find all the answers in these pages..**10**

Day Itineraries

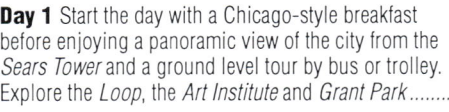

Three itineraries that give you the full-bodied flavor of Chicago and its environs with suggestions on where to eat along the way.

Day 1 Start the day with a Chicago-style breakfast before enjoying a panoramic view of the city from the *Sears Tower* and a ground level tour by bus or trolley. Explore the *Loop*, the *Art Institute* and *Grant Park*................**21**

Day 2 Stroll along *Michigan Avenue*, otherwise known as the *Magnificent Mile*, passing landmark buildings like the *Wrigley Building* and the *Water Tower*. Savor a real Chicago deep-dish pizza for lunch before heading to *Navy Pier* for an afternoon of fun. Take a leisurely dinner cruise on *Lake Michigan* later in the evening...**28**

Pages 2/3: rooftops of the Windy City

Day 3 Take a trip to the pretty suburb of *Oak Park* to visit the *Home and Studio* of America's most renowned architect, *Frank Lloyd Wright* as well as the birthplace of *Ernest Hemingway*. Browse in specialty stores in the afternoon, and then see a play with dinner in the evening...**35**

Pick & Mix Itineraries

Eleven different suggestions for visitors with more time to spare and to help experience everything this dynamic city can offer.

1 *Lincoln Park* is much more than a park. Visit the *Conservatory* and the free *Zoo*, and take a boat ride on the *Lagoon*. Ride a highwheel bike in the hands-on History Gallery of the *Chicago Historical Society*. To round off this range of diverse activities, take your pick from a list of the best comedy clubs in America.............**42**

2 *North Michigan Avenue* is home to Chicago's glitziest stores including three vertical shopping malls. Put on your comfiest shoes and prepare to shop till you drop **45**

3 The *Field Museum*, the *Aquarium* and the *Adler Planetarium* are conveniently located together between the downtown area and the lake. Examine dinosaur skeletons, take in a dolphin show and explore the mysteries of the skies. Bring along a picnic to eat in the park **48**

4 The *Picasso* sculpture in the Loop, and what it all means, is a source of controversy. Make up your own mind. *City Council* meetings are open to the public. Relax with a tasty sandwich and lunchtime entertainment in the *Daley Center*..**50**

5 The *Museum of Science and Industry* is a short trip away from the downtown area. Exhibits include a German submarine from World War Two and a 16-foot pulsating model of a heart. *Hyde Park* and the *University of Chicago* are just around the corner..................**54**

6 *Architecture Tours* abound. Marvel at the most noteworthy buildings by foot, bus, bike or boat on the river – the choice is yours..**57**

7 Blues fans are spoiled for choice, with a cluster of clubs in the north, and *Buddy Guy's Legends* and the *New Checkerboard Lounge* to the south..............................**58**

8 An *Untouchables Tour* catapults you back into the gangster-era. Have lunch later at *Michael Jordan's Restaurant* or *Hard Rock Cafe*...**60**

9 Sports fans take their pick between *Comiskey Park* or *Wrigley Field* for baseball, the *United Center* for basketball and hockey or *Soldier Field* for football...............**62**

10 *River North* has the largest concentration of art galleries outside Manhattan. Browse, then have lunch at *Carson's The Place for Ribs*. Finish up by touring the *Merchandise Mart* **64**

11 Join the audience of *The Oprah Winfrey Show* and see America's number one talk show host in person **65**

Shopping, Eating Out & Nightlife
Everything you need on what to buy and where to buy it, how to eat well, and where to hit the town **68–78**

Calendar of Events
Events worth watching and catching up with throughout the year in Chicago **79–81**

Practical Information
All the information you need for a smooth visit, including places to stay and how to get around..............**82–92**

Maps
Around Chicago...................**4**		**Lincoln Park** **42**
The Loop............................**18**		**Museums**.............................**48**
Mag Mile and Navy Pier **28**		**Hyde Park**............................**54**
Oak Park..............................**35**		**CTA System**..........................**84**

Pages 8/9:
Buckingham
Fountain

Index and Credits 94–97

History & Culture

When French explorers Father Jacques Marquette and Louis Jolliet first canoed into the area in 1673, they encountered marshland that the Indians called *Checagou,* meaning wild onions. But its potential was clear – its access to waterways in all directions made the location a prime spot for trading.

In 1779, Jean Baptiste Point DuSable established the first trading post on the north bank of the Chicago River at what is now Michigan Avenue, becoming the first non-Native American to settle here. In 1803, US soldiers built Fort Dearborn. In 1825 the Erie Canal created a new water route between Chicago and the East, and settlers from the East arrived in even greater numbers. In 1837, Chicago, with a population of around 4,000, was recognized as a city. Its central location helped it grow as a rail center and the opening of the Stockyards in 1865 made it a hub of activity for the cattle industry as well. Immigrants were drawn to the city, and by 1870 the population had grown to 300,000.

Builders and Planners

A defining moment in Chicago's development occurred the night of October 8, 1871, when Mrs O'Leary's cow kicked over the lantern in her barn, starting a fire that came to be known as the Great Chicago Fire. There's no way to be sure the legend is accurate, or if that poor cow has unjustly taken the blame all these years, but a fire did start that Sunday night in the barn behind the O'Leary cottage. For two days, it spread through the city, fueled by wooden buildings, blowing winds, and a Midwest drought that had lasted since summer. The fire burned a path through 2,600 acres, leaving 300 dead, 100,000 homeless, and 18,000 buildings destroyed. Damages were estimated

The Great Chicago Fire of 1871

at $200 million. The city was destroyed. But, instead of being defeated, Chicagoans came through with their can-do spirit. They used this catastrophe as an opportunity for rebirth; a chance to start over and rebuild the city. In the words of Joseph Medill, then publisher of the *Chicago Tribune*, 'We have lost money, but we have saved life, health, vigor, and industry. Let the watchword henceforth be, Chicago shall rise again!'

And rise it did. Because of the open canvas the city now presented, architects were attracted from other parts of America and Europe, and swarmed to be part of rebuilding the city of Chicago. Past building mistakes were gone, and fireproof brick and steel frames became the building materials of choice. The City Council decreed that no wooden buildings could be put up in the central business district.

Renowned architect Frank Lloyd Wright

Chicago was still growing as an industrial center. Big buildings were required to support the growth, and the architects were up to the challenge. The skyscraper was born, and Chicago's skyline started to develop.

From the 1870s to the 1890s, the foundations of modern architecture and construction were created by the men who came to be considered the Chicago School of Architecture: Jenney and Mundie, Root and Burgee, Adler and Sullivan, Holabird and Roche, Burnham and Root, H. H. Richardson, and Frank Lloyd Wright. They worked for and with one another, and their names can be found on many buildings throughout the Loop.

Although building started in the 1870s, nothing of note remains from before the 1880s. In 1883 William Jenney, an engineer, invented the first skyscraper construction building using a metal skeleton to support exterior walls, a design still used today. His earliest surviving metal frame structure built in 1891 stands at the southeast corner of State and Van Buren streets in the Loop. Chicago currently has three of the world's 10 tallest buildings, The Sears Tower, the Amoco Building, and the John Hancock Center.

The rich architectural tradition continued. Mies van der Rohe escaped Germany and came to Chicago in 1938 where he lived and worked until his death in 1969. He spent the first 20 years at what would become the Illinois Institute of Technology, training a generation of architects. His belief that less is more can be seen in his glass and steel high-rise apartments built without mortar and free

Chicago Board of Trade

of exterior decoration. Helmut Jahn is a present-day architect contributing much to the city of Chicago. His work can be seen in the Xerox Centre (1980), the art deco revival addition to the Chicago Board of Trade (1982), the State of Illinois Center (1985), and the United Airlines terminal (1987).

During the period of rapid development following the Great Chicago Fire, someone luckily recognized the value of the lakefront, someone willing to fight to maintain it. In the 1890s, retailer Montgomery Ward was upset over plans to build in Grant Park. He began a 20-year crusade relying on an old clause in the city code that decreed the lakefront should be forever free and clear. Although the clause had previously been ignored, Ward fought through the courts until he prevailed. Park officials wanted to put buildings on the land; aldermen thought the downtown lakefront should be used to bring revenue to the city. At one point, Ward counted 20 proposals for the land. Although his reasons may not have been entirely altruistic – he was growing unhappy with the view from his offices on Michigan Avenue – Ward's open lakefront concept has benefited generations of Chicagoans and visitors.

By 1909, the city had a building plan. The *Plan of Chicago* was developed by Daniel H. Burnham and it called for lakefront parks, a boat harbor in the lake, the transformation of Michigan Avenue into a high-grade shopping street, and the construction of a wide thoroughfare (the Eisenhower Expressway) running west from downtown, among other ideas. While not all of the suggested projects were ultimately implemented, the spirit of the planner who decreed 'Make no little plans' has shaped the city.

In 1922, an international contest was held for the design of the Tribune Building. When Raymond Hood and John Mead Howells' winning Gothic design was built, it increased interest in the area north of the Chicago River, leading to the construction of the Michigan Avenue Bridge, and ambitious commercial development along the stretch of Michigan Avenue. This is the strip frequently referred to as the Magnificent Mile.

City of Neighborhoods

Chicago is often referred to as a city of neighborhoods. Since the development of Chicago began, people came to Chicago from all over the world, settling in areas where they had something in common with those already living there. Each neighborhood has its own feeling, its own style. The Loop is the oldest and most central. They must have put something in Bridgeport's water in 1932, for since then many Chicago mayors have hailed from this neighborhood five miles southwest of the Loop. Originally settled in the 1830s by Irish laborers who came to help construct the Illinois-Michigan Canal, Bridgeport is also one of the stockyards neighborhoods, which for 100 years served as the primary employer on the South Side. Back of the Yards, Canaryville, McKinley Park and Gage Park are other working-class neighborhoods whose residents once worked in the stockyards.

The communities are often ethnic enclaves. There's Greektown and Chinatown (Cermak Rd and Wentworth Avenue, first settled by Chinese immigrants around 1912), best-known for their restaurants. Pilsen is a predominantly Mexican-American community and Little Village is a Mexican community near 26th and Kedzie. Heart of Italy is one of the oldest city neighborhoods consisting mostly of Italians from the Tuscany region, with many family-owned and operated restaurants. Andersonville is a Scandinavian area of restaurants, bakeries and shops that grew from the Swedish farms of the 1840s.

Beverly, the largest urban historic district containing 3,000 buildings with national register status, calls itself the Village in the City. Hyde Park was established in the 1850s with the Illinois Central Railroad connecting it to the city and is home to the University of Chicago. Lincoln Park refers to both the park and the neighborhood around it. Lakeview finds you sitting in the bleachers at Wrigley Field, munching on hot dogs and trying to catch a fly ball.

People identify themselves by their neighborhood. They don't say they live in Chicago; they might say that they live in Pullman, an 1880s planned community for employees of the Pullman sleeping-car firm;

Street music

Richard J. Daley

or in Old Town, probably best known by inhabitants for its summer art fair and Second City Comedy Club.

Chicago continues to grow and flourish. While the city of Chicago has well-defined boundaries, the Chicagoland area includes a good number of suburbs, such as Oak Park, where most of architect Frank Lloyd Wright's work is concentrated. As the growth continues, towns which were formerly considered to be out in the country are now seen as part of the Chicagoland area.

Politics for the People

As the city grew, so did its political arena. It has been said that Chicago's favorite pastime is politics. In the first mayoral election, early settler John Kinzie, a natural choice for the city's first mayor, was defeated by William B. Ogden, a former New York legislator who came into town in the 1830s to dump some land a relative had bought sight unseen. But after making a handsome profit on the deal, he stayed and got rich. As his fortune grew, the city benefited. He built the first railroad, still around today as the Chicago & North Western. By 1856, Chicago was the hub of 10 railroad lines and earning a reputation as America's crossroads.

In the summer of 1932, Chicago hosted both the Democratic and Republican presidential nominating conventions. Franklin D. Roosevelt won the Democratic nomination, and broke tradition by flying to Chicago to address the convention. In his speech he pledged a New Deal for the American people, thus introducing the name for the government programs that would be created to fight the Depression. In 1933, Anton J. Cermak, the 36th mayor of Chicago, was shot by a bullet intended for President-elect Roosevelt, while the two were talking.

Cermak is credited with (or blamed for) establishing the Democratic machine. He brought together diverse factions, using clout and patronage to reward his supporters and punish his opponents, and it was he who began the Democratic hold on the mayor's office that continues to this day. In 1954, party leaders endorsed Cook County clerk, Richard J. Daley, who was elected mayor in 1955.

Chicago is a city of Democrats, and one of the best known is Richard J. Daley, Da Boss, one of the last of the old-time political bosses, who served a record six terms as mayor, each time elected by huge margins. He was mayor for 21 years, and jointly held the title of Cook County Democratic Party Chairman, which gave him tremendous power. Although best known for his colorful personality and strong Democratic machine, he used his power to make

Chicago a better place. It was under his direction that McCormick Place was built, helping Chicago expand as a convention center. Daley is also due credit for the construction of major expressways and O'Hare Airport. We can thank him for Chicago's nickname and reputation as 'the city that works'.

Daley's oldest son followed his path into politics, serving in the Illinois State Senate and as State's Attorney of Cook County, before being elected mayor in 1989. Richard M. Daley, still mayor of Chicago at the time of writing, continues the legacy of improving the city. McCormick Place has been expanded, Navy Pier has been renovated, and the new international terminal has opened at O'Hare. He won the right to host the National Democratic Convention for the first time since the anti-war riots at the 1968 Convention, which helped restore the city's tarnished reputation.

Community policing has been developed to help keep neighborhoods safe and the greening of the city has resulted in the planting of countless trees. Chicago is getting to look more like its motto, *Urbs In Horto*, City in a Garden.

Greening of the city

Machine gun politics

Chicagoans would rather the rest of the world forgot about gangland boss Al Capone, but no record of the city's history would be complete without the story of his ruthless and bloody reign.

It was after World War 1 that Chicago's focus of power shifted from industrialists to politicians. While heirs to Chicago's great retailing and meatpacking fortunes ensconced themselves on the North Shore, crooked politicians and bootleggers plundered the city. For these were the Prohibition years, from 1920-1933, when a constitutional amendment outlawed alcoholic beverages.

Chicago in general boomed during the Roaring Twenties. Fortunes were made in the rising stock market. More big buildings went up. Flappers danced on speakeasy tables. Legal nightlife sparkled with dozens of vaudeville houses and legitimate theaters that featured both local groups and touring professional troupes. Most people tolerated crime as a part of everyday life as long as it wasn't one of their relatives or friends who was cut down in the latest careless crossfire among rival hoodlums. So the bootleggers slugged it out and more than 400 gangsters were killed over five years, including seven in the 1929 St Valentine's Day Massacre.

A one-time speakeasy bouncer who graduated to running brothels, Capone built a vast bootlegging empire that included importing whisky from Canada and operating his own beer breweries right in the middle of Chicago. To keep his operations going, he made the bribery of officials at every level an everyday fact of life that still plagues Chicago today.

Capone was short and pot-bellied and not particularly physically imposing. But he was a crudely brilliant and cunningly brutal organizer who ruled through a combination of fear and rewards, stick and carrot. Those who did what he wanted could get rich quickly, those who refused requests could get dead even more quickly. He often made his points in a dramatic way, sending out carloads of gunmen with nonmusical violin cases or interrupting a black-tie banquet to kill a disloyal lieutenant with repeated blows with a baseball bat. Capone is listed in the *Guinness Book of Records* for the highest gross income ever accumulated by a private citizen in a single year: $105 million in 1927, when he was 28 years old.

Capone was finally brought down by a group of federal agents, led by Eliot Ness and known as the Untouchables for their refusal to take bribes. Unable to pin murder or even bootlegging directly on the crafty Capone, Ness and his men instead went after the gangster for failing to pay taxes on his millions in illicit gain. Capone was convicted and went to prison. He died in 1947, quietly, in

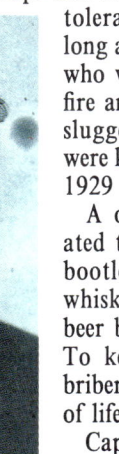

Al Capone

Historical Highlights

PRE-1800 The Pottawattomie Indians traded here and called it Checagou, meaning wild onions.

1673 Explorer Louis Jolliet and Jesuit missionary Father Jacques Marquette were the first non-Native Americans to reach Chicago.

1779 Jean Baptiste Point DuSable established a trading post on the north bank of the Chicago River at what is now Michigan Avenue.

1803 Federal soldiers built Fort Dearborn at what is now Michigan Avenue and Lower Wacker.

1812 Indians burned Fort Dearborn and massacred most of the settlers.

1818 Illinois became a state.

1825 The Erie Canal opened, making it possible to travel by water from New York to Chicago.

1831 The first bridge linking the North and South sides of Chicago was built over the Chicago River.

1837 Chicago was incorporated as a city. William B Ogden became the first mayor of the city with a population of 4,170.

1848 The Chicago Board of Trade was formed.

1865 The Stockyards opened.

1871 The Great Chicago Fire demolished much of the city.

1889 Celebrated architect Frank Lloyd Wright built his Home and Studio in Oak Park.

1890 Chicago's population passed the one million mark.

1892 The prestigious University of Chicago was founded.

1892 The elevated train line around the downtown business area opened.

1893 Chicago hosted the Columbian Exposition which was attended by 27 million people.

1900 The flow of the Chicago River was reversed away from Lake Michigan so that sewage would not contaminate the lake's drinking water.

1909 The City Plan was presented by architect Daniel Burnham calling for preservation of the lakefront.

1931 Tony Cermak laid the groundwork for Chicago's Democratic political machine.

1931 Crime boss Al Capone was convicted of federal income tax evasion and sentenced to prison.

1933 Chicago hosted the Century of Progress World's Fair, drawing crowds of 39 million.

1934 Bank robber John Dillinger was gunned down outside the Biograph Theater by federal agents.

1951 Carl Sandburg won the Pulitzer Prize for poetry.

1955 Richard J Daley was elected the city's mayor.

1955 O'Hare Airport opened.

1966 The Reverend Martin Luther King Jr founded the Chicago Freedom Movement, which led to Operation Breadbasket and PUSH.

1967 The Picasso Sculpture was given to Chicago.

1968 Riots erupted at the Democratic Convention.

1974 Sears Tower opened as the world's tallest building.

1976 Mayor Daley died in office.

1979 Jane Byrne became the first, and so far only, woman elected mayor of Chicago.

1983 Harold Washington became the first African-American mayor.

1989 Richard M Daley won a special mayoral election.

1992 Flooding of the underground tunnel closed the Loop.

1996 Chicago hosted the Democratic Convention for the first time since the riots in 1968.

1997 Chicago Bulls basketball team, led by Michael Jordan, became five-time NBA world champions.

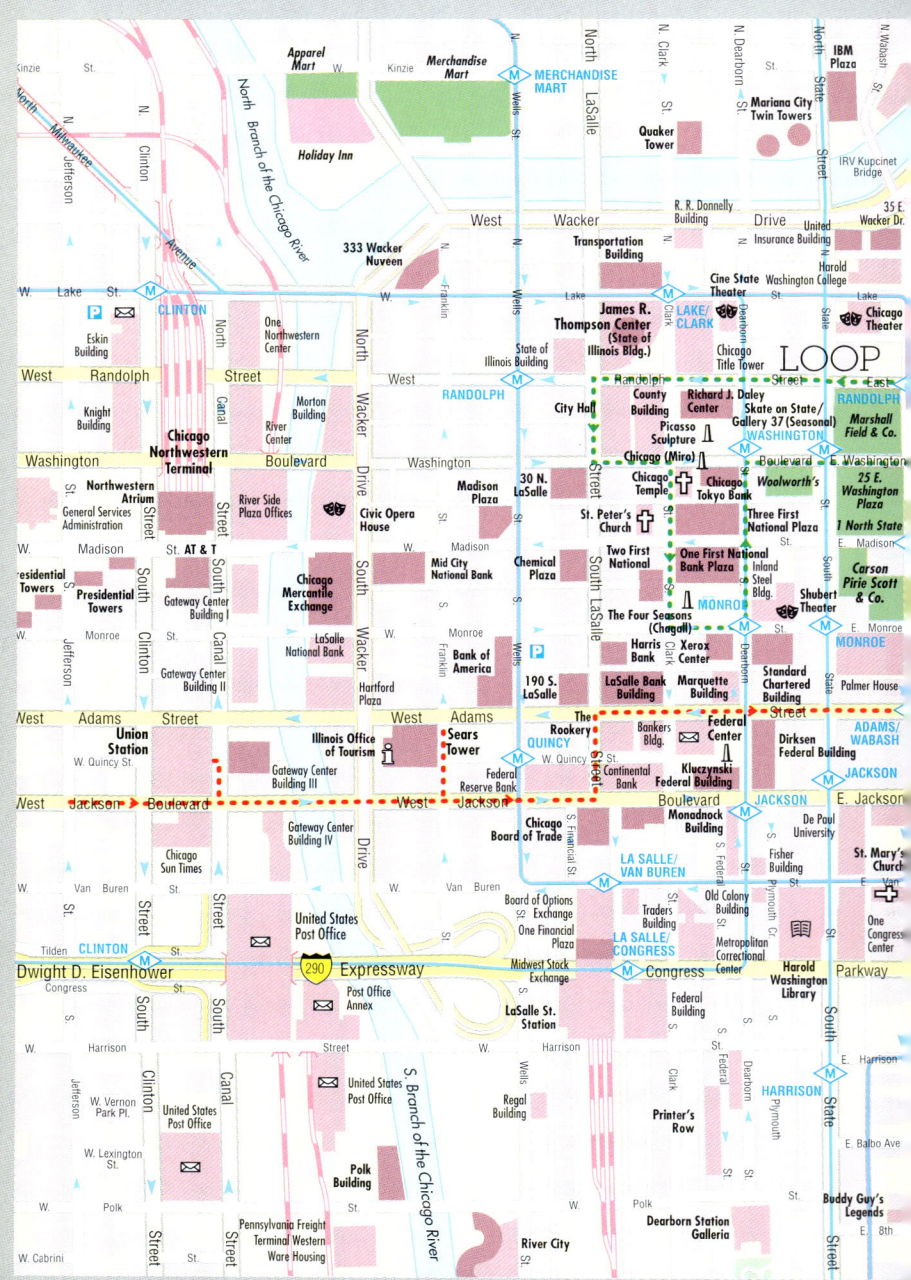

Day Itineraries

The downtown area will be your base for most of these full-day activities, with one day spent in a suburb to see another side of the city. A car isn't necessary in Chicago. The itineraries are planned primarily for walking, with public transportation available when you've had enough. Even the trip to the suburb of Oak Park can be done on public transportation.

Because you'll be doing a lot of walking, the following points are worth noting:

Remember the lake is to the east, and you won't get lost.

Wear comfortable shoes. There's a lot to see and the sidewalks aren't cushioned yet.

Keep this number handy: 836-7000. It's the Chicago Transit Authority (CTA) helpline. They usually answer promptly, and will tell you how to get from one place to another by bus or train. Distances between bus stops are short: look for the blue and white bus stop sign. Note that the signs are sometimes missing, possibly liberated by souvenir hunters – just ask if you're unsure.

Most of the museums offer one free day a week. If these don't fit your schedule, console yourself with the fact that at least you won't be obliged to sharpen your elbows – admission-free days are *very* popular.

Remember these plans are flexible. If you have no interest in seeing the trading activities at the Chicago Board of Trade, skip it. You'll have more time to wander the Art Institute. If the Art Institute is more time indoors than you want to spend, cut it short and head to the lake. I've suggested alternatives along the way.

Please refer to the price guide in Eating Out for restaurant prices in this section.

Finally, to help you blend right in, remember that Chicagoans pronounce their town as *Chicawgo*, not *Chicahgo*.

Lions guard the Art Institute

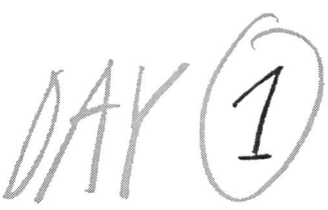

South Loop: Sears Tower to the Art Institute

Breakfast at Lou Mitchell's, then take in a panoramic view of the city from Sears Tower Skydeck. Hop on a one-hour bus or trolley tour. Discover a few historical buildings on your way to lunch at the Berghoff. Explore the Art Institute in the afternoon, then stroll through Grant Park. Enjoy an evening play or concert. *See map on page 18–19.*

–To start: Since you'll be doing quite a lot of walking today, I would recommend taking a cab or bus to Lou Mitchell's, since this is the farthest point. You can hail a cab outside your hotel, or call the CTA (Chicago Transit Authority) for the most direct bus route from your hotel to Jackson & Jefferson.–

The organized will have already ordered tickets to the performance of their choice for tonight, or plan to attend a free Grant Park Concert, where reservations are not needed. If you're more of a, shall we say, *spontaneous* type, call to see if there's a free concert tonight, tel: 742-4763, or stop by Hot Tix (see Nightlife for addresses) to see what shows they can offer you. (Or call Hot Tix, tel: 1-900-225-2225. Watch out though – it'll set you back $1/minute.) Make a dinner reservation at the restaurant of your choice (see suggestions and telephone numbers later in itinerary). If attending a Grant Park Concert, either get there early enough to grab a chair or take something comfortable to sit on.

In 1892, a series of elevated train tracks were installed in downtown Chicago. The trains made a loop around the central downtown district be-

Taking the 'El' in The Loop

fore continuing to outlying regions. **The Loop** refers to the area enclosed by the tracks, the central business district of the city, although Chicagoans use the terms Loop and downtown interchangeably. Today is spent on the south end of the Loop, starting

21

at the western edge and heading in the direction of the lakefront.

If you get an early enough start, there's a restaurant considered a Chicago institution just a few blocks west of the Loop, where I recommend you start your day. **Lou Mitchell's** ($), located at Jackson & Jefferson (565 W. Jackson), Monday to Saturday 5.30am–3pm, Sunday 7am–3pm, is not a fancy restaurant, but may just be the best spot for breakfast in Chicago. It's a busy, fun place where everything is homemade and fresh: the French toast is made of thick slices of homemade Greek bread, the waffles are delicious and the omelettes, a house specialty, are jumbo-sized and fluffy. Pastries are made in their bakery on the premises. Did I mention the double yolk eggs? Have a cup of coffee – they claim to have the world's finest. Don't worry if there's a line (there almost always will be!); it goes fast, and they pass out little boxes of Milk Duds to the female customers who are waiting. Breakfast is served all day and they also open for lunch. Remember to bring cash, as they don't take credit cards or checks.

Sears Tower

When you leave Lou Mitchell's, turn right, and you'll be walking east on Jackson. Turn left on Canal Street and enter **Union Station**, 210 S. Canal Street, on your left, for a quick look at the station. Amtrak trains arrive and depart from here. Built in 1917, Union Station is everything a train station should be. The waiting room, for example, is spacious and has a 10-story dome overhead.

Return to Jackson, and continue east. The bridge you cross takes you over the South Branch of the Chicago River. Looking ahead, you won't be able to miss **Sears Tower**. After three years of building, Sears Tower opened in 1973 as the world's tallest building, with 110 stories. The Petronas Towers in Kuala Lumpur, Malaysia, with only 88 floors, has now officially taken the title. However, there's some grumbling as to how accurate that is, since the spire was included in the measurements, and Sears counts only the actual building in their measurements.

The **Sears Tower Skydeck** entrance is on your left. It's open 9am–11pm daily, with the last ticket sold at 10.30pm. Arrive early to beat the long line. Admission charge includes an eight-minute movie, *Over Chicago* – skip it if you're short of time. Make sure you're given a map, then enjoy the exhibits on the way to the elevator, which will take you on a 70-second ride up to the breathtaking view from the Observation Deck on the 103rd floor. As you move around the floor, a recorded message tells you what's visible in that direction. Use the map to check out landmarks – on a clear day you can see 40-50 miles, including four states (Illinois, Indiana, Michigan and Wisconsin). Enjoy the view!

Trading place

Now that you've seen where everything is, take a tour to see the same sights up close, and get a feel for the layout of the city. Bus or trolley tours are available outside Sears Tower. They visit much the same places and cost close to the same amount, so decide if you prefer to ride the trolley or the double decker bus, and climb aboard. Tours last an hour or a little longer.

When you return to Sears Tower, continue east on Jackson. Time for a snack? Drop into one of the four bakeries between Sears Tower and the Chicago Board of Trade building. It's only a few blocks, but keep in mind the last presentation at the Board of Trade begins at 12.30. If you're not interested in visiting the Board of Trade, then you're on your way to lunch.

The **Chicago Board of Trade**, 141 W. Jackson, was founded in 1848 to promote and monitor Chicago commerce. Traders originally traded actual sacks of grain. The development of quality standards allowed trading of quantities for a specific grade rather than the actual sacks, which in turn led to futures trading, an agreement to buy or sell in the future.

Drop by the Visitors Gallery, tel: 435-3500, of the trading room on the fifth floor to observe actual trading, Monday to Friday 8am–1.15pm. Each pit is a circle of traders interested in buying or selling a particular agricultural commodity, using an open auction system. It looks like chaos with all the hand gestures and yelling, but pick up an explanatory pamphlet, and if possible hear the presentation (available in English, Korean, Italian, Japanese, Portuguese, Spanish, Russian or French), and see the short film (available in all except Italian). Free admission.

As you exit on Jackson Blvd, do not turn onto Jackson, but walk straight ahead, staying on the right side of the street. You are now going north on LaSalle Street. This is the chief financial district in Chicago. As you head for lunch, you can get a quick look at a couple of landmark buildings. Before entering the **Rookery** at 209 S. LaSalle, turn back to get a look at the building you just left.

The graceful Rookery

The striking Flamingo sculpture

The 45-story Chicago Board of Trade building at the foot of LaSalle was the tallest building in Chicago when it was designed in 1930 by Holabird and Root and was given landmark status in 1967. Give Ceres, the Roman goddess of grain and harvest, a wave – she's the 31-foot (9m) statue on top of the building.

Enter the Rookery, a 12-story office building created by architects John Root and Daniel Burnham in the 1880s with a skylit lobby (the lobby was remodeled in 1905 by Frank Lloyd Wright). Notice the ceiling, the spiraling staircases, and the splendor of marble, glass, and ironwork. Walk through the lobby, veering towards your left as you enter, then exit on Adams Street.

Turn right as you leave the building, and continue walking east on Adams. As you reach Dearborn Street, the **Federal Center and Plaza** is on your right, where you'll come face to face with a striking orange sculpture by Alexander Calder: **Flamingo**, dedicated in 1974. You want to turn the other way (left) on Dearborn to reach the **Marquette Building**, 1405 South Dearborn Street. This building, designed by Holabird and Roche in 1894, is an example of the Chicago School of Architecture's use of steel columns to usher in the era of the modern skyscraper. Note the interesting door as you go in. The unusual lobby is a rotunda in honor of Père Marquette, credited with discovering Chicago together with Jolliet. Mosaic panels depicting scenes from early Chicago history surround the lobby. Bronze panels over the main entrance continue the theme. Sculptured heads above the elevator doors of early French explorers and Native American chiefs are on both the first and second floors.

Return to Adams, and go east half a block to **The Berghoff Restaurant** ($$), tel: 427-3170, 17 W. Adams Street, another Chicago institution. Again you'll probably wait in line, but it moves quickly. This bustling, noisy restaurant with its oak paneled walls has an olde-worlde atmosphere and a menu offering German classics and American cuisine. Try the schnitzels or the pot roast along with seeded rye bread and some of their excellent signature beer, on offer since Prohibition ended. Sure, the fare is heavy, but you're doing a lot of walking today. You'll burn those calories off in no time at all. Note one of the Berghoff's claims to fame on display inside – the first city liquor license ever issued.

The Berghoff Restaurant

Art Institute

Continue east on Adams Street to the **Art Institute**. Located on Michigan Avenue at the end of Adams Street it's recognized by the lions on each side of the entrance. Stop by the information desk for a map of the museum: it's best known for its French Impressionist collection, but that's just the start: you'll also find Post-Impressionist, Modern, Egyptian, Chinese, European, and Indian here, as well as frequent special exhibitions. Look out, too, for the reconstruction of the trading floor of the old Chicago Stock Exchange.

If you have children with you, it might be smart to start on the lower level at the Children's Museum – this is also where you'll find the fascinating must-see Thorne Miniature Rooms. Admission charge; children half price. Tuesday free to all. Additional cost for special exhibitions. The gift shop is worth a browse and can be entered without paying the admission charge. Hours: Monday and Wednesday to Thursday 10.30am–4.30pm; Tuesday 10.30am–8pm; Saturday, 10am–5pm; Sunday noon–5pm.

If you have time when you leave the Art Institute, walk south on Michigan Avenue to the corner. This is the northwest corner of **Grant Park**, site of many of the city's summer events and thus a favorite spot for Chicagoans. In addition to Taste of Chicago (catch it in late June/early July, admission free, just pay in vouchers for your chosen taste) this is where various music festivals are held, free of charge. **Petrillo Music Shell** is at the corner of Columbus Drive and Monroe Street and holds free concerts up to four nights a week in summer.

You'll pass a statue of Abraham Lincoln on your way to **Buckingham Fountain**, given to Chicago by Kate Sturges Buckingham in memory of her brother Clarence. Dedicated in 1927, it is modeled on one of the fountains at Versailles. The fountain operates May 1 to October 1, with a color light show nightly from 9–11pm. This is a relaxing spot for sitting down and enjoying the scenery, soft drink or ice cream cone in hand. Wondering where **Lake Michigan** is? You're only a block away. Head east from the park.

Have some dinner before the event you've chosen for tonight. There are three good restaurants very near the Schubert Theater, and within walking distance of any of the theaters except the Mayfair. Less than a block west of the Schubert are **Nick's Fishmarket** ($$$$), tel: 621-0200, One First National Plaza, an expensive but excellent seafood restaurant; or **Italian Village** ($$-$$$), tel: 332-7005, 71 West Monroe Street, a more moderately priced alternative which is actually three restaurants. Reservations are required.

A third restaurant is a little closer to the lake if you're staying for a Grant Park concert or attending the Goodman or Orchestra Hall. **Miller's Pub** ($-$$), tel: 263-4990, 134 South Wabash, is famous for its ribs, and offers everything from sandwiches to complete dinners. Reservations are accepted, and the restaurant is open until 3.30am if you prefer to eat after the concert or theater. At time of writing, Orchestra Hall, tel: 294-3000, 220 South Michigan, is undergoing a major facelift with plans to include a restaurant for concert and theatergoers. If you prefer to skip a big meal, stop by one of the vendors near Buckingham Fountain – Gino's East and the Buckingham Cafe & Grille serve pizza, grilled sandwiches, pasta salads and pesto chicken.

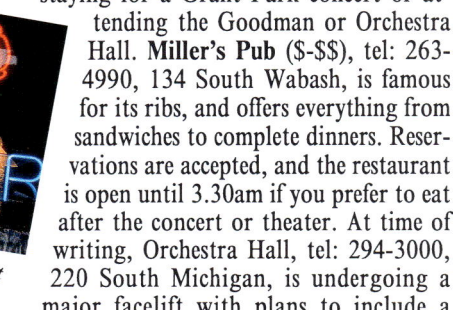
Shelling out at Nick's Fishmarket

If you're lucky enough, you'll be here on a night of a **Grant Park Music Concert** at Petrillo Music Shell in Grant Park, on the corner of Columbus Drive and Jackson Blvd, featuring the Chicago Symphony Orchestra and Chorus or a guest artist. These concerts have been a Chicago tradition since 1935. The outdoor setting is perfect with the lake on one side and the city skyline on the other, and the price is pretty perfect too – it's free. It's a good, fun place to picnic in the summer sunshine if you want to grab some carry-out instead of going out to dinner.

Note that you're not allowed to bring alcohol into the park, though this apparently has less to do with protecting the good citizens of Chicago from themselves than topping up the city's coffers, as you can often buy beer from approved vendors once you're inside. Devious, un-civic-minded types – certainly no one connected with this guide – have been known to repackage wine and beer in soda bottles in order to foil the cops, who will confiscate anything remotely resembling alcohol and add it, frustratingly, to a growing booze mountain by the park entrance. Particularly daring if irresponsible individuals bribe their offspring to divert the cops' attention while they surreptitiously retrieve their confiscated beer.

Either way, a park concert is hard to beat as a way to unwind at the end of your first day. Bring something to sit on. If there is at the end of your first day. Bring something to sit on. If there is no concert or if you would prefer to go to the theater, you should have already purchased your tickets, although some of the theaters offer discounted tickets an hour or two before showtime. Hot Tix is a source for same-day half-price tickets (see Nightlife for phone number and addresses of booths).

Some of the nearby theaters: **Shubert Theater**, tel: 977-1700, 22 W. Monroe, is one of the few remaining remnants of the Loop's once thriving theater district, offering Broadway presentations by touring companies; **Goodman Theatre**, tel: 443-3800, 200 South Columbus, Chicago's oldest and largest residential theater, offers a mix of classical revivals, musicals and new works. During the Christmas holidays, a presentation of *A Christmas Carol* is a well-attended annual event. And, although the performances are usually sold out to subscription sales, the **Chicago Symphony Orchestra** performs at **Orchestra Hall**, tel: 294-3000, 220 South Michigan Avenue.

A few blocks further south is the **Mayfair Theater** in the Blackstone Hotel, tel: 786-9120, 636 South Michigan. *Shear Madness* has been playing here since 1982. If this is your destination, consider **Prairie** ($$$), tel: 663-1143, 500 South Dearborn, with its Midwestern cooking, for dinner. Or to keep things nice and simple, eat at the Blackstone Hotel – it has a restaurant called **The Grill** ($$), tel: 427-4300.

Think about returning to Grant Park afterwards to enjoy the spectacle of Buckingham Fountain all lit up. It's an impressive sight, and well worth the effort.

Hoping for luck on the lake

DAY 2

The Magnificent Mile and Navy Pier

Starting at the Michigan Avenue Bridge, explore the stretch of Michigan Avenue known as the **Magnificent Mile**. See landmark buildings including the Water Tower that survived the Chicago Fire. Have lunch at the restaurant where deep dish pizza was invented. Then spend the afternoon and evening at Navy Pier, possibly taking a dinner cruise.

—To start: If you'd like to take a dinner cruise, make reservations on the Spirit of Chicago, tel: 836-7899, or Odyssey, tel: 630-990-0800. Ask about dress requirements.—

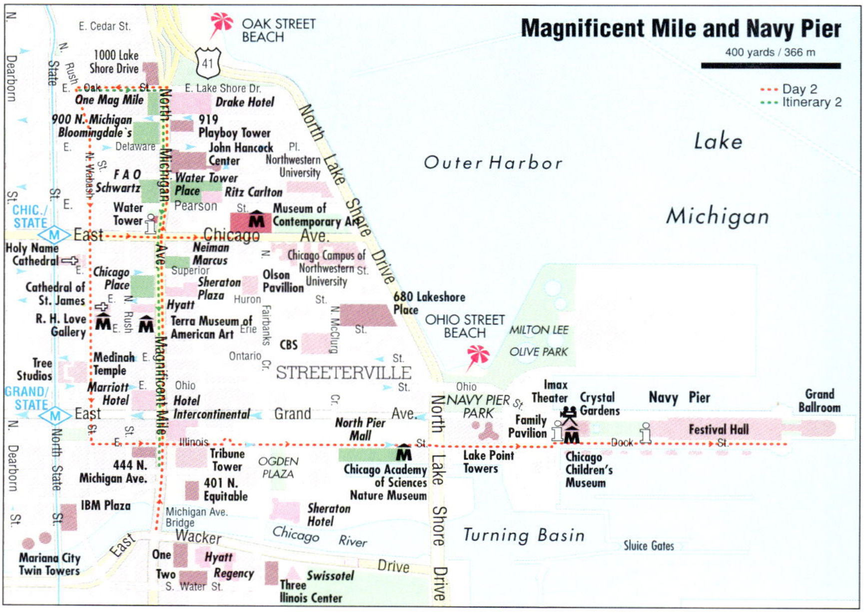

Walk or take a bus or cab to the **Michigan Avenue Bridge**. The bridge is an appropriate place to start a day in Chicago because it symbolizes so much of Chicago's history. The four pylons at each corner of the bridge represent major events – the discovery by Marquette and Jolliet, the pioneers who settled here, the Fort Dearborn Massacre of 1812, and the rebuilding of the city after the Great Fire of 1871. This was the site of Fort Dearborn, and the

approximate spot where DuSable built the first permanent structure when he settled in Chicago. This *trunnion bascule* bridge, with its two leaves that pivot up and down to let tall ships pass, is one of 52 movable bridges over the Chicago River. It is also one end of the stretch of Michigan Avenue that realtor Arthur Rubloff referred to as the **Magnificent Mile**, a name that caught on so well that even the nickname Magnificent Mile has a nickname, Mag Mile. That's where you'll head when you leave the bridge.

After looking at the bridge and the Chicago River, glance north. The terracotta building on the west side of the street at 400 North Michigan Avenue is the **Wrigley Building**. This is the corporate headquarters of the Wrigley chewing-gum empire. Rising above the Chicago River is the widely recognized clock tower. The Wrigley Building comes into its own at night, when it's brightly illuminated, a result of William Wrigley's request to make it resemble a luscious birthday cake.

The Wrigley Building

The bridge is also a prime position for surveying the next building of interest on this walking itinerary, **Tribune Tower** on the east side of the street. In 1922, Tribune publisher Robert McCormick held an international contest to design the world's most beautiful office building and the winning design, by prominent New York architects Raymond Hood and John Mead Howells, was completed in 1925.

As you approach Tribune Tower, you will notice the southwest corner of the building is a studio behind windows where you can watch the live broadcast of WGN Radio. WGN is owned by the Tribune, and takes its call letters from the newspaper's motto, World's Greatest Newspaper. As you approach the entrance on Michigan Avenue, note the stones from famous places such as the Parthenon, Notre Dame of Paris, Westminster Abbey and the Great Wall of China. Similar fragments are embedded all around the base of the building. The Gothic arch leads to a lobby in which the walls are inscribed with messages supporting patriotism and freedom of the press. There is an adjacent Tribune Store.

As you stroll down Michigan Avenue, you'll pass **Viacom Entertainment Center**, one of the

Jazz on Michigan Avenue

Nike Town

newest additions to the Mag Mile featuring television memorabilia, and come across Burberrys, Cartier, Crate and Barrel, and Sony as you continue north. If you're traveling with a kid who wants to be like Mike, you won't be allowed to walk by **Nike Town**, 669 North Michigan Avenue. The store combines merchandise and exhibits; there are store maps available by the entrance.

Just across the street is the **Terra Museum of American Art**, tel: 664-3939, 666 North Michigan Avenue, a small intimate museum that's free on Tuesday, and charges admission on other days. It has somewhat erratic opening hours – 10am Wednesday to Saturday, noon Tuesday and Sunday, and closed altogether Monday – so it may not be open when you go by.

The next block offers Tiffany and **Chicago Place**, a vertical mall featuring Saks and Ann Taylor. There's a bakery inside if you need to stoke up before lunch. Pick up a copy of their complimentary monthly city guide for current listings of exhibits, theater and sports schedule.

Continue to the historic **Water Tower**, 800 North Michigan, the oldest structure in the city, built in 1869. The Water Tower and the **Pumping Station** directly across the street are rare specimens, survivors of the Great Chicago Fire. This landmark currently houses one of Chicago's **Visitors Centers**. Stop in for answers to any questions you might have, and to get information on any sights you're interested in. Pick up a *Chicago Calendar of Events*, and the *Chicago Gallery News* which includes a map of art gallery locations and information on openings. There is also a Hot Tix booth here.

Water Tower

You are at a pivotal spot in the day. If you like modern, avant-garde works, go east one block to the **Museum of Contemporary Art**, tel: 280-2660, 220 East Chicago, featuring art from 1945 to today. Open Wednesday and the first Friday of the month 10am–9pm; 10am–6pm other days. Admission charge. Children 12 and under free. Free Monday.

If you are traveling with small children, you might consider skipping the museum and continuing a half block north on Michigan to

FAO Schwartz, a fabulous, larger-than-life toy store. Or if you won't have another chance to shop or get back this way, **Water Tower Place** is directly across the street from FAO Schwartz. Just north of Water Tower Place is the **John Hancock Center**, tel: 888-875 VIEW (8439), 875 N. Michigan. Although we've scheduled it for a possible night visit, if that doesn't fit your plans and you weren't able to visit the Sears Tower Skydeck, you might like to take advantage of the **Observation Deck**, on the 94th floor, while you are so close. (*See page 34.*)

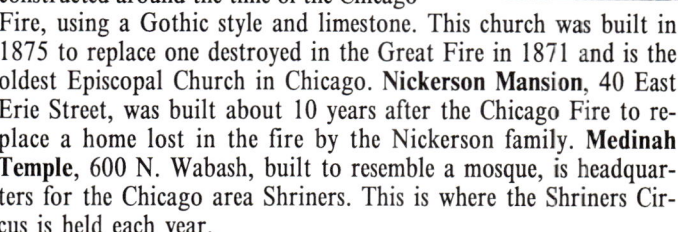

John Hancock Center

Although you haven't walked the entire Magnificent Mile at this point, since you'll see the rest of it if you do some shopping later (*see Pick & Mix 2*), and since you want to save plenty of time for Navy Pier, especially if you have children with you, plan to turn west here onto Chicago Avenue. However, if you won't be back in this direction, and you would like to complete the Magnificent Mile (and your legs haven't given way) continue north on Michigan Avenue to Oak Street, West on Oak Street to Rush, south on Rush to Wabash, then continue south on Wabash.

Otherwise, return to Chicago Avenue (Water Tower), walk two blocks west to Wabash, and turn left. **Holy Name Cathedral**, 730 Wabash, is the primary church of the Roman Catholic Church in the Chicago Archdiocese. It was built in the 1870s. **Episcopal Cathedral of St. James**, 65 E. Huron, is typical of the churches constructed around the time of the Chicago Fire, using a Gothic style and limestone. This church was built in 1875 to replace one destroyed in the Great Fire in 1871 and is the oldest Episcopal Church in Chicago. **Nickerson Mansion**, 40 East Erie Street, was built about 10 years after the Chicago Fire to replace a home lost in the fire by the Nickerson family. **Medinah Temple**, 600 N. Wabash, built to resemble a mosque, is headquarters for the Chicago area Shriners. This is where the Shriners Circus is held each year.

Turn left on Ohio to **Pizzeria Uno**, known locally simply as Uno's ($) tel: 321-1000, 29 East Ohio, located in a Victorian mansion turned pizza parlor. Chicago is famous for its deep-dish (pan) pizza, and this is where it all began. In 1943, the late Ike Sewell lined a deep pan with a flaky crust, threw in some mozzarella cheese, added layers of sausage and fresh tomatoes and, hey presto, the pizza that Chicago came to love was invented. This is a popular spot with Chicagoans and tourists, and the restaurant is small. If the wait is longer than you like, backtrack around the corner to

Fun for all at Navy Pier

Pizzeria Due, or Due's as it's called ($) tel: 943-2400, 619 N. Wabash. Although not the actual restaurant where deep dish pizza was started, it's a sister restaurant, and the pizza is identical.

Hunger pangs taken care of, it's time to head to **Navy Pier**. At this time of the day, Navy Pier offers free trolleys to the pier on weekends throughout the year, and daily in summer, which you can catch on Grand Avenue, a block south of Uno's. The trolley travels from Navy Pier west on Grand to State Street, one block south on State to Illinois, to return east to the pier.

Do note that while the city also has sightseeing trolleys, only the Navy Pier trolleys on this route are free.

If there is no trolley or you don't want to wait, go another block south to Illinois and take either a #29 or a #65 CTA bus to Navy Pier. Or if you're in the mood for a walk, just go east about 7 blocks along Illinois which will take you right there.

If you're traveling with a teenager, consider a brief stop at **North Pier**, 435 East Illinois Street. It's on the way to Navy Pier if you're walking, and just a couple of blocks west of the pier if you took the bus or trolley. Your teenager will doubtless appreciate the break from sightseeing, and there are plenty of fun shops to keep you occupied while he or she plays video games and rubs elbows with others the same age. Don't miss the **City of Chicago Store**, where in addition to the regular souvenir items you can purchase actual used items like street signs or a brick from Chicago Stadium or the old Comiskey Park. They also carry a variety of Chicago maps and books. The **Chicago Academy of Sciences**, tel: 871-2668, has a nature museum with hands-on activity for the younger crowd. While children have a lot of fun here, it's not actually as big as the museum for children at Navy Pier. There is indoor miniature golf, however, good for a rainy day. Monday to Friday 9.30am–

4.30pm, Saturday 10am–6pm, Sunday noon–6pm. Admission charge. Children under three free. Everyone free Tuesday.

Save plenty of time for the next stop. There's no admission, but there are charges to some specific attractions.

You can spend the rest of the day and evening playing at Navy Pier, tel: 595-PIER (7437), 600 E. Grand Avenue, a renovated Chicago landmark with over 50 acres of shops, attractions and restaurants. Navy Pier first opened in 1916. Through the years it operated as a municipal pier, a military facility, and a branch campus of the University of Illinois, until falling into disuse in the early 1970s. In the early 1990s, a major redevelopment project was undertaken. Over $150 million in restorations and improvements were made before its re-opening celebration in 1995.

It sounds like a cliché, but there is truly something for everyone. Spend your time here wandering and enjoying. You'll want to trawl the pier inside and out to find what appeals to you, but I'll just give you an idea of what's available. As you approach, you'll go through gardens and past fountains; the first building brings you into the **Family Pavilion**. Stop at the information counter for a map. The Family Pavilion houses the **Chicago Children's Museum** with more than a dozen permanent and changing exhibits, programs and workshops. This hands-on museum dedicated to curiosity and creativity is a favorite of the pre-teen set. Admission charge. Tuesday to Sunday, and Monday in summer, 10am–5pm. Free family night Thursday, 5pm–8pm.

The 440-seat **IMAX Theatre,** admission charge, is also in the Family Pavilion. You'll feel you're actually in the movie once you put on the 3D glasses with Surround Sound.

There is an indoor **Crystal Gardens**, year round retail shops, and in summer additional vendor carts outside. You'll also want to head outside for a ride on the Carousel and the Ferris Wheel, for yet another, 150ft (45m) view of the city. A reflecting pond converts to an ice rink in winter. The **Skyline Stage** is a 1500-seat outdoor venue hosting musical acts and entertainers.

To the south of the Family Pavilion is **Dock Street**. This is where you will find outdoor vendors and street performers from magicians to mimes. From Dock Street you can reach **Festival Hall** which offers several shows throughout the year such as an Art Show, Flower Show, and County Fair. There's a **Beer Garden** which needs no explanation. Continue to the end of the pier for a great view and to see the **Grand Ballroom**. There are also a number of restaurants and a food court.

Dock Street is where the dinner

Go for a spin on the Ferris Wheel

cruise boats are docked, too. There are two primary dinner cruises ($$$$) currently available, each around three hours long. Both include a full course meal, sightseeing, dancing and live entertainment. In addition to the dinner cruises there are also less expensive lunch cruises, midnight cruises, and Sunday brunch cruises. If you've made a reservation for a dinner cruise, leave plenty of time to get to the boat – it's unlikely to wait for you! Note that they leave at different times depending on the day of the week, so check the time when you make your reservation. The two cruise lines are **Spirit of Chicago**, tel: 836-7899, and **Odyssey**, tel: 630-990-0800.

If a boat ride isn't appealing, or the prices aren't to your liking, the skyline view is still great from the pier, and there are plenty of restaurants to choose from ranging from fine dining at **Riva** ($$$), for seafood and Italian dishes, to more moderately priced restaurants to a food court with tables inside or out.

Check to see if tickets are available for the **Skyline Stage** performance at the box office, tel: 595-5290, or Ticketmaster, tel: 559-1212.

When you're ready to call it a day, either catch the free trolley, call the CTA for information on the bus to take you to your hotel, catch a cab, or start walking west. If you still have some energy and time, board a #66 CTA bus west to Chicago and Michigan (Water Tower), then walk 2 blocks north to the John Hancock Center, 875 N. Michigan Avenue. The **Hancock Observatory**,

Cruisin' in style

tel: 1-888-875 8439, underwent a $2.5 million renovation in 1997. In addition to stunning 1,000ft- (305m-) high views of the city and lake, the Observatory offers virtual reality technology in *Windows on Chicago*. There's also a Skywalk 94 storys above street level where you can actually step out to a screened-in area, 9am–midnight daily. Admission charge. Children aged five and under are admitted free.

If you'd like to see the same view without visiting the Observatory, have a drink at **The Signature Room at the 95th** in the John Hancock Center. Drinks are on the pricy side but look on it as the cost of renting a table with an incredible view and it'll seem a great bargain. Try to arrive early enough to secure a window table, but not so early that you'll have left before it gets dark – the view by night is stunning. Hint to female visitors: don't leave without a visit to the ladies' restroom, where the best view of all is to be had. (Sorry, guys.)

Another alternative to end your day is a **carriage ride** along Michigan Avenue from the Water Tower. Again, wait until the lights of the city are on. Catch a ride at Michigan Avenue and Huron, or Michigan Avenue and Pearson.

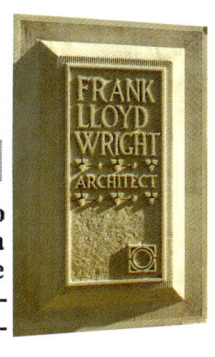

Frank Lloyd Wright's Oak Park

Take a ride to the sought-after suburb of Oak Park to visit Frank Lloyd Wright's Home and Studio, enjoy a walking tour of interesting architecture, and visit the Wright-designed Unity Temple. Drop by the Ernest Hemingway Museum. Shop in the specialty shops. See Shakespeare in the Park.

—To start: although easily accessible by public transportation, if you do have a car, this is the day you might like to use it. Parking is plentiful and inexpensive, making a refreshing change from downtown. Take the Eisenhower Expressway (I 290) to Harlem. Go north on Harlem to Lake, east on Lake to Forrest, left on Forrest ½ block. There's a parking lot right next to the Visitors Center.—

If you're using public transportation, here's your chance to do something few tourists do — take the El. Board the CTA Green Line (Lake Street), heading either north or west (do not board a south- or eastbound train. There are five stations downtown where you can catch the Green Line: on Wabash at Adams, Madison, or Randolph, or on Lake Street at State or Clark. Get off the train at the 'Oak Park' stop. Walk a block north to Lake Street, then a few blocks west to Forrest. If you'll be staying in Oak Park for the evening, make reservations for Village Players, tel: 708-848-1500, or Shakespeare in the Park, tel: 708-524-2050 (including perhaps a box dinner) if you haven't already purchased your tickets. Make a dinner reservation at Philanders of Oak Park, tel: 708-848-4250, if that's part of your plans.

This western suburb, covering under 5 square

The architect's playroom, designed for his six children

miles, is one of the oldest in the Chicago area and offers a very different setting and pace from downtown. City-dwellers planning on an eventual move to the suburbs to raise a family often aspire to living in prestigious, family-oriented Oak Park – conversely, young singles seeking a frenetic social life in Oak Park are more likely to find a elephant in their morning cereal.

The primary reason to visit Oak Park is for the architecture as this is where Frank Lloyd Wright introduced his Prairie-style dwellings. Oak Park has a higher concentration of Wright-designed structures than anywhere else in the world. There are 25 in Oak Park, and an additional eight in neighboring River Forest. Wander through this outdoor museum of architecture for a first-hand experience.

There are three main tours available; the Frank Lloyd Wright Home and Studio, a walking architectural tour, and Unity Temple. They can be taken in any order, depending on the time you start. If coming by train, make your first stop the **Oak Park Visitors Center**, tel: 708-848-1500, 158 Forest Avenue (just north of Lake Street). Daily 10am-5pm. Closed December 24-25 and January 1. They have a gift shop, and knowledgeable attendants familiar with Oak Park. At this time, Oak Park's Children's Museum is closed while it looks for a new home. If you're interested in the museum, ask at the Visitors Center.

About 3 blocks north, at the corner of Forrest and Chicago, is the **Frank Lloyd Wright Home and Studio**, tel: 708-848-1976, 951 Chicago Avenue. This was the home and workplace of America's most renowned architect and he used it as his personal designing laboratory for the first 20 years of his career. Guided tours

Wright's 'little jewel', Unity Temple

of this National Historic Landmark start in the **Ginko Tree Bookshop**, located in what was the Wright family garage built in 1911 behind the House and Studio. They are offered Monday through Friday at 11am, 1pm, and 3pm, weekends from 11am–4pm continuously. Groups of 10 or more are required to make reservations. There is an admission charge.

See the house that Frank built in 1889 when he was only 22 years old. This is the home where Wright and his family lived, and the studio where he worked, from 1889 to 1909. He and his wife raised six children here and the children's play room is rather intriguing – be sure to notice the unusual piano treatment. Wright wanted the house's natural materials to come into the living space and felt that the heart of the house is the hearth, so there are several fireplaces with exposed masonry. Horizontal lines are predominant; since the Midwest is flat plains, Wright felt the buildings here should follow the same pattern. Although the house he lived in is not Prairie style, it was in his studio that the Prairie design was developed. This tour lasts 45 minutes to one hour.

On weekends you can take a guided tour of the historic district at 10am, noon, and 2pm. Self-guided audio tours are available daily from 10am–3.30pm. These cassette tours, which take

Wright Home and Studio

approximately 1–1½ hours, are offered in English, Spanish, German, Japanese, French and Italian. There are advantages to both types of tour: with a guide you have someone to answer questions, and they are fairly knowledgeable; a cassette allows to set your own pace. Both types are well done, though neither takes you inside the homes. One of the buildings you see from outside, the Moore-Dugal, is open for tours (additional charge) on weekends.

After returning your cassette player to the Ginko Tree Bookshop, which is also a gift shop, take a well-deserved lunch or ice cream break at **Petersen's Restaurant & Ice Cream Parlor** ($), tel: 386-6131, 1100 Chicago Avenue, Monday to Friday 10am–11pm, Saturday and Sunday 8am–11pm. It's nothing fancy, but the fact that it's been in business for 75 years should tell you something. In addition to its regular menu, Petersen's features four daily specials, and its own bakery and nationally famous ice cream. Return to the Moore-Dugal Tour Home on Forrest if you would like to take that tour.

The **Moore-Dugal Tour Home**, tel: 708-848-1500, 333 Forrest Avenue, was Frank Lloyd Wright's first independent assignment in Oak Park after he left the offices of Adler and Sullivan. He was approached by Nathan G Moore with a commission for a period home, completed in

Frank Lloyd Wright

One of 25 houses designed by Frank Lloyd Wright

1895. After a fire destroyed much of the house in 1922, Frank Lloyd Wright returned to redesign and rebuild the home. Tours are available Friday and Saturday 10am–4pm, Sunday noon–4pm. Admission charge; tickets available at the Visitors Center.

Unity Temple, tel: 708-383-8873, 875 Lake Street, is the third main tour. This lovely National Historic Landmark, designed in 1905, is the only major public structure from Frank Lloyd Wright's early Prairie School days that's still used today. The architect referred to the temple as his 'little jewel'. The revolutionary concrete building looks nothing like a typical church structure. Self-guided audio cassette tours that include both interior and exterior features are available Monday to Friday 1–4pm; from Memorial Day to Labor Day expanded hours are 10am–4pm. Guided tours given Saturday and Sunday 1, 2 and 3pm. Charge for tours.

Now it's time to make some choices. If you've had enough touring and just want to relax, **Austin Park** is a pleasant park across from the Oak Park Visitors Center. Stop in Starbucks around the corner on Lake Street for a cappuccino.

If you're interested in writer Ernest Hemingway, continue east on Lake Street to Oak Park Avenue, and turn left. About a block and a half up is the **Hemingway Museum**, tel: 708-848-2222 (for museum and birthplace), 200 N. Oak Park Avenue, where you can explore the impact that an Oak Park upbringing had on one of America's greatest authors. The museum's exhibits and videos cover the first 20 years of Hemingway's life, highlighting four themes: family life, the role the outdoors played in his development, his education in the Oak Park public schools, and his experiences in World War I. The museum shop sells books, gift items, posters and videos.

Continue another block to visit **Hemingway's Birthplace**, 339 North Oak Park Avenue, where the Nobel-prize winning author was born on July 21, 1899. This was the Victorian home of Hemingway's maternal grandfather where Hemingway lived for the first six years of his life with his extended family. Displays include historic photographs documenting family history, a facsimile of Hemingway's first book, created when he was two years old, memorabilia from the family and a video presentation on the family's history. A combined ticket can be purchased for museum and birthplace.

Or maybe you'd rather shop. The stores in the vicinity of Lake and Oak Park Avenue are called **The Avenue**. There are a number of specialty stores and restaurants, including **Cafe Winberie** ($), 151 North Oak Park, with a varied menu and large portions, and **Geppetto's ($), 113 North Oak Park, for Italian dishes. **Lake Street** is the downtown strip of Oak Park and is lined with stores. There's a pedestrian mall on Marion Street between Lake Street and the train tracks, which includes **Antiques Etc. A Mall**, with over 20 antique dealers, and many little shops and bakeries with yummy food.

If you will be staying in Oak Park for evening activities, or would like to eat here before returning downtown and are looking for something a little ritzy, **Philander's of Oak Park** ($$), tel: 708-848-4250, 1120 Pleasant Street (in the Carleton of Oak Park), is just off Marion Street, south of the train tracks. This hotel dining room offers fine dining specializing in seafood. There's also a sidewalk cafe in summer, and live jazz Monday to Saturday; it's handily on the way to Village Players.

There are a couple of long-established performing groups in Oak Park. **Village Players**, tel: 708-848-1500, 1010 Madison Street, has been performing for over 35 years. They perform five different shows between September and May, as well as a summer show, on Friday and Saturday evenings at 8pm. They also offer an occasional Sunday matinee at 1pm and Thursday 8pm show. Tickets can be purchased at the box office which opens an hour before the show. Call to see if there will be a performance the day you will be there.

Oak Park Festival Theater, tel: 708-524-2050, performs Shakespeare under the stars in Austin Gardens from June until August. Performances are Tuesday to Thursday at 8pm in Austin Park. Tickets can be purchased at the entrance or pre-purchased by charge card. This is an outdoor performance, so bring a blanket or rent a chair. Box dinners are available, but these have to be ordered and paid for ahead of time.

I should mention there is a certain amount of controversy in the neighborhood regarding tourists. On the one hand there are the residents who welcome the tourists (some doubtless seeing dollar signs), on the other there are those who are totally disenchanted with the idea of hordes of people traipsing nosily through their neighborhood and who would be thrilled never to have to come face to face with a gaggle of camera-touting strangers again. Readers of this guide are much too well-behaved to need a reminder to respect both the locals' property and privacy.

When ready to return downtown, go back to the same place where you arrived. At the risk of sounding like an over-anxious parent, do be careful to follow the signs to downtown Chicago to be sure you are on the right side of the tracks to board the train. It wouldn't be the first time someone has ended up hurtling in the wrong direction.

The Wright stuff

1. Lincoln Park

Visit the Conservatory, the Zoo and the Historical Society in Chicago's largest park.

Lincoln Park refers to Chicago's largest park featuring a zoo, conservatory, lagoons, paddle boat rides, gardens and a museum, as well as the neighborhood surrounding it, which combines tranquil tree-lined avenues and busy commercial streets. It's a couple of miles north of downtown, but is readily accessible by bus. Call the CTA for directions from where you are staying. If you would like more information about the Lincoln Park area, call the **Chamber of Commerce** (tel: 773-880 5200). If your plans for the evening take you north of Lincoln Park Zoo, consider reversing the following route and taking the bus to North Avenue to start.

Take the 151 bus to Fullerton Avenue to visit **The Conservatory**, 2400 North Stockton (Fullerton & Stockton), tel: 742-7736, a free indoor garden at the north end of Lincoln Park. Hundreds of plants are displayed in four large greenhouses, each in their own natural environment, and you can wander among them to a background of classical piano music. The Fern House includes cycads, the oldest plants from the Mesozoic Period – about 135 million years old. The Cactus House holds cacti and succulent plants in a southwestern desert landscape while the Palm House is the place to see rare orchids from many countries, banana trees, rubber trees, and of course palms. The Show House

holds four major shows each year: the Azalea Show in February or March, an Easter show in Spring, a Chrysanthemum show in November, and the Christmas show during the Christmas holidays in December. Open daily 9am–5pm.

Enjoy the formal gardens in front of The Conservatory, as you walk to the zoo entrance directly to the east. There is no admission charge to **Lincoln Park Zoo,** 2200 North Cannon Drive, tel: 742-2000, which is open 9am–5pm, 365 days a year and offers an easy, relaxing and fascinating day out with or without kids. The zoo, founded in 1868 with a gift of two swans from New York's Central Park, provides naturalistic settings for over 1,000 animals living here, including nearly 30 endangered species. The zoo follows the school of thought that rather than display animals in cages, natural habitats must be reproduced to ensure the preservation of the animals.

Lincoln of Lincoln Park

Pick up a free zoo map at the entrance to help you find particular exhibits, or just stroll the grounds, gradually working your way south. The map helpfully includes the times for scheduled animal feedings and daily programs.

The **Pritzker Children's Zoo and Nursery** located near the west entrance is a favorite area of the zoo, and not just with the kids. Large bays of windows let you watch baby animals being cared for by zoo personnel (and treated like real babies – a popular sight is a monkey in diapers). Zoo staffers often take small animals out of their cages for visitors to hold or pet.

The newest addition to the zoo is the Regenstein Small Mammal-Reptile House which houses small animals in the environments of four continents. Visit the Great Ape House to see the largest collection of lowland gorillas in the United States living in a naturalistic setting. Ask to be introduced to the unusually wise and gentle gorilla Frank, who has made something of a name for himself over the years as a foster dad to abused and orphaned kid gorillas. Watch the polar bears as they enjoy their large pool and walk around the pool until you come to the underwater viewing windows. It's quite a sight to see them swimming underwater right next to the windows. There are penguins, koalas, and all the other animals you'd expect to find. In addition to being a great place to visit to see the animals, the zoo hosts occasional interesting diversions such as Caroling to the Animals at Christmas time, and the Spooky Zoo Spectacular for Halloween.

Walking south from the Regenstein Small Mammal-Reptile House or west from the Antelope and Zebra area you'll see the **South Pond** (often referred

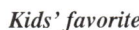

Kids' favorite

Chicago Historical Society

to as the Lagoon), a relaxing place for a stroll or a picnic. You can rent paddle boats in the summer to take a leisurely boat ride around the lagoon. Hungry? **Cafe Brauer** and **Ice Cream Shoppe** are next to the paddle boat rentals.

The next stop heading south is an unusual feature. The **Farm in the Zoo** allows city children who might otherwise grow up believing milk comes from the same source as 7-Up and Coca-Cola to see what happens down on the farm. Watch a cow-milking demonstration in the dairy barn. Watch as other farm chores are performed in one of the barns for livestock, poultry, horses, or the main barn.

Still walking south, enjoy a couple of blocks of open park land – a nice area to picnic, rest or let the kids run around. Go through the viaduct running under the street at the south end of the park. The big building on your right is the **Chicago Historical Society**, 1601 N. Clark (Clark Street at North Avenue), tel: 642-4600. History takes a new turn at the society, which was founded in 1856, making it the city's oldest cultural institution. It features hands-on exhibits and artifacts that recount Chicago's history from the 1700s through today.

See what life was like for the pioneers in the Illinois Pioneer Life Gallery. Walk into an early fur traders' cabin, feel the beaver pelt and see the cooking kettle. Climb aboard Chicago's first locomotive. Unless you've heard enough about it, watch a movie about the Chicago Fire and be grateful you were born a century later. Visit the hands-on History Gallery where you can ride a highwheel bike or play with 19th century toys. Special events are offered during the year. Open Monday to Saturday 9.30am–4.30pm, Sunday noon–5pm. Admission charge. Free Monday.

You could do a lot worse than hang out in Lincoln Park for the evening. Three comedy clubs, Second City, Second City E.T.C., and Zanies Comedy Club (*see Nightlife*) are just a few blocks west of the Chicago Historical Society on Wells Street in the area called Old Town. If you're going to a comedy club, you might enjoy a steak at **O'Brien's Restaurant & Bar** ($$), 773-787-3131, 1528 North Wells, just a block south of the clubs. O'Brien's has a piano bar and is also open for Sunday brunch.

Other evening possibilities include a blues club (*see Pick & Mix 7*), or a theater, such as **Victory Gardens Theater**, tel: 773-871-3000, 2257 North Lincoln, featuring world premier works by contemporary playwrights. If you like the idea of one of these evening activities, consider reversing the route to save your legs. For a dinner treat, try **Un Grand Cafe** ($$), tel: 773-348-8886, 2300 N. Lincoln Park West (a block west of The Conservatory). Patio dining is available in warm weather at this popular bistro overlooking Lincoln Park. Superb food, and French wines available by the glass.

2. The Magnificent Mile

Visit the outstanding stores on Oak Street and Michigan Avenue. This is the day to shop till you drop. *See map on page 28.*

To see how an area earns a name such as Magnificent Mile, start on Oak Street. Although not actually on Michigan Avenue, Oak Street is at the head of Michigan Avenue between Michigan Avenue and Rush Street, and shouldn't be missed. It's a very elite block of shops located in restored brownstone buildings built by Chicago's wealthy following the Great Chicago Fire. How many streets have their own valet parking? Start with a makeover from Marilyn Miglin, pick out a designer outfit, get matching shoes, purse, hat, jewelry, glasses, choose a leather or fur coat, have your hair and nails done or find just the right perfume all at different boutiques. Wishful thinking? Window shop like the rest of us – it's still (sort of) fun.

Chicagoan shoppers beat the cold

The head of the Mag Mile is the **Drake Hotel**, 140 East Walton. If possible, plan your shopping trip so you can have afternoon tea in the lobby of the Drake. If not, stop in to see the marble and oak lobby complete with fountain.

North Michigan Avenue has three vertical malls, as well as a variety of wonderful shops along the street. Coming from Oak Street or the Drake Hotel, the first mall you will come to is the **900 North Michigan Shop**, tel: 915-3916. This six-level mall has over 70 shops, 10 restaurants, and two cinemas and makes a very elegant walk even if you're not buying. A fountain in the middle of an open center creates a very spacious feeling. Merchandise here is generally sophisticated and expensive – Bloomingdale's is the anchor store – but you will also find Henri Bendel, Gucci, J. Crew, and dozens of other opportunities to bankrupt yourself in style. Atlas Galleries and Gallery Lara are also located here. The Four Seasons Hotel is in the same structure. Monday to Thursday 10am–7pm, Friday 10am–8pm, Saturday 10am–6pm, Sunday noon–6pm.

Continuing south, the **John Hancock Center** is on the left. Go down the steps to the Garden Plaza that includes restaurants and shops. If you're hungry, L'Appetito Cafe and Deli, or the Cheesecake Factory, a restaurant, bakery and bar, both pleasant stops with outdoor seating, would welcome you dropping by. The Chicago

A street named desire

Water Tower Place

Architecture Foundation has a branch here, if you need to make arrangements or pick up information on architecture cruises. You might find it useful to know there's a Chicago souvenir shop inside the John Hancock building.

Cross Chestnut Street to reach **Water Tower Place**, 835 North Michigan Avenue, tel: 440-3166, the second, and probably the best known of the malls. Prepare for the glitter and crowds. This is a very popular upper-crust shopping destination, featuring seven levels with over 100 trend-setting stores, eateries, and cinemas. Take the escalator past waterfalls and foliage to reach the elevators: the recommended way to see everything is to take one of the glass elevators to the top floor, and work your way down.

Water Tower Place is anchored by Marshall Field's on the north and Lord & Taylor on the south; you will also find Louis Vuitton luggage, Bigsby & Kruthers, Merrill Chase Galleries, jewelry at Christian Bernard, Abercrombie & Fitch, and FAO Schweetz, a candy store on a big scale. The Ritz Carlton Hotel, tel: 266-1000, is above the east wing of the complex. Monday to Thursday 10am–7pm, Friday 10am–8pm, Saturday 10am–6pm, Sunday noon–6pm.

Directly across the street at 840 North Michigan Avenue is FAO Schwartz, tel: 587-5000. The oversized toys in the window let you know that this is a place for small kids but of course it's a great shopping experience for big kids too. Extravagance seems to be the operative word and bring either your checkbook or your will-power because it's hard to resist. Pick up a copy of the Chicago edition of the popular board game, Monopoly.

An old-fashioned ice cream parlor is nestled amid all the modern glitz. **Ghirardelli Chocolate Shop and Soda Fountain**, 830 North Michigan, is the perfect place to restore your energy. And don't you deserve it! Crossing Chicago Avenue brings you to **Neiman Marcus** at 737 North Michigan Avenue, tel: 642-5900. You can't miss the 2-story arched glass doorway leading to this complete department store carrying designer apparel.

South of Superior on the west side of the street is where you'll find the third mall, **Chicago Place**, 700 North Michigan Avenue, tel: 226-7710, with more than 50 shops and restaurants in an 8-level mall. Saks Fifth Avenue is the anchor store with departments on seven levels and you can also shop at Talbots, Ann Taylor, The Body Shop, or Hello Chicago. The eighth level is the Garden Food Court surrounding an indoor garden. Chicago Place offers a concierge service at the entrance on the first level, where they provide city wide information on events, and will assist you with reservations. Baby strollers and wheelchairs are available. Monday to Friday 10am–7pm, Saturday 10am–6pm, Sunday noon–5pm.

On the east side of the same block you'll see Florsheim and Joan and David. If you are looking for fine crystal, shimmering silver or diamond jewelry, Tiffany's is just the store, located at 715 North Michigan Avenue. This is also the block containing Brooks Brother and Enzo Angiolini, as well as the Allerton Hotel. The Avenue Cafe and Restaurant in the hotel provides a serene setting for breakfast or lunch. Coming up is **Nike Town**, 669 North Michigan Avenue, so you are now in the area you passed on Day 2. But that was merely looking, whereas this little outing is more along the lines of retail therapy!

South of Huron you'll find The Gap, Elan Furs, Cole-Haan for shoes, Nike, Sony, Burberrys, Crate & Barrel. There is also Fannie May, Wedgewood, Waterford, Crabtree & Evelyn, and Cartier. Viacom Entertainment is the new kid on the block featuring television and movie paraphernalia.

Back on Michigan continue south for H2O, Levis, Eddie Bauer, Timberland, Forgotten Woman, Hammacher Schlemmer & Co for ev-

The Place for shopping

ery gadget imaginable, and the previously mentioned Tribune Store. If you still haven't had enough, there's also a shop in the NBC Tower, east of Tribune Tower, or cross the bridge and continue south on Michigan Avenue.

3. Grant Park Museums

Three great museums very close together – the Field Museum, John G. Shedd Aquarium, and the Adler Planetarium. Spend a short time at each, or pick your favorite and spend more time exploring it. This would be a good day for a picnic in Grant Park.

Getting to these museums is easy. If you're traveling from State Street downtown or North Michigan Avenue, hop aboard a 146 bus. From anywhere else, call the CTA on tel: 836-7000 for how to get around.

Chicagoans love their world-class museums almost as much as tourists do. To make the setting more inviting, the city has recently undergone a major project on this stretch of land once used for Chicago's Century of Progress Exposition. Northbound Lake Shore Drive has been relocated to the west of the Field Museum. Now, instead of having to cope with the traffic of a busy street, visitors can peacefully stroll from one museum to another in a campus setting, called appropriately Museum Campus. The city also came up with the idea of offering a free trolley service between the museums, which certainly saves some walking. Right now it isn't clear whether this is a temporary or permanent arrangement, but Chicagoans hope it will continue in the future. Wondering about the large building directly south of the Field Museum? It's Soldier Field, where the Chicago Bears play football.

If you plan to visit the Oceanarium and haven't pre-purchased tickets, make the Aquarium your first stop to see if any same-day tickets are available. Otherwise, visit the museums in any order.

John G. Shedd Aquarium, tel: 939-2438, 1200 South Lake Shore Drive, features a global collection of sea life representing more than 650 species. The center of the Aquarium features the Coral Reef, a 90,000 gallon exhibit which is 12ft (4m) deep and 40ft (12m) in diameter. A scuba diver

The Aquarium – exploring on a grand scale

hand-feeds the sea turtles, fish and eels. Check the schedule for times. This is a popular activity so head to the Coral Reef a few minutes early so young children can get close enough to see. Branching out from the Coral Reef in the center are corridors of individual tanks.

The Aquarium has always attracted enormous crowds, but the addition of the Oceanarium in 1991 swiftly endowed it with even more pulling power. The **Oceanarium** recreates a Pacific Northwest coastline and includes a 1,000-seat auditorium where you can watch shows featuring dolphins in the largest indoor marine mammal pavilion in the world. Here's where you'll see whales, dolphins, sea otters, and harbor seals. A colony of penguins are in a separate exhibit which recreates a Falkland Islands environment. Visit the popular underwater viewing gallery.

There is an additional charge to visit the Oceanarium, but children two and under are free. Free admission to the Aquarium Thursday; there will still be a charge for the Oceanarium, and visitors still need a ticket. You'll receive a timed ticket, and can enter only at the time printed on your ticket, but can stay as long as you like. The time on the ticket is an enter time, by the way, not a show time. Tickets can be purchased at the box office or from Ticketmaster by phone, tel: 559-0200. Advance purchase is recommended. John G. Shedd Aquarium features the Soundings Restaurant, tel: 986-2286, the Bubble Net Food Court, and several gift shops. Open daily 9am–6pm in summer. The rest of the year, the museum closes at 5pm on weekdays. Closed Christmas and New Year's Day.

The **Field Museum**, tel: 922-9410, Lake Shore Drive at Roosevelt Road, was founded in 1893 to house the natural history collection gathered for the Columbian Exposition. The original museum opened in 1894, then moved to this, the largest marble building in the world, in 1921. The building was partially maintained with funds donated by Marshall Field, founder of the department store.

If you have children who can't get enough of dinosaurs, this is the place you want to be. You'll be greeted by the largest mounted dinosaur in the world. Examine dinosaur skeletons,

Past lives at the Field Museum

including a four-story tall Brachiosaurus. The museum has an exhibit which takes you inside Ancient Egypt, where you can descend into an Egyptian tomb and see real mummies. Test your own pulling power – try moving a three-ton stone block as the pyramid builders did.

Explore the history of evolution of life on Earth from the earliest single-celled DNA-based form of life through those in the Age of Dinosaurs. Then continue from the dinosaurs' extinction to the evolution of man. Travel the Pacific South Sea Islands, and watch glowing lava flow. Touch a meteor, feel an anteater's tongue, smell a dinosaur's breath. Here you can go around the world and travel through time, all in a day. The Field Museum has gift shops and a McDonald's, as well as an indoor picnic area.

Starry-eyed

Admission charge, reduction for children 3-17, seniors and students with ID. Free Wednesday. Open 9am–5pm daily.

Adler Planetarium, tel: 922-STAR (7827), 1300 South Lake Shore Drive. Although everyone calls it the Planetarium, its full name is the Adler Planetarium and Astronomy Museum, which gives a more accurate description of what it has to offer. There are three floors of exhibits and activities in astronomy and space exploration. There are telescopes, both usable and historical, and models of the planets. You can even find out what you would weigh on different planets in the Space Transporters and go home with a whole new perspective on those pounds you thought you needed to shed.

An escalator travels through a field of stars and darkness to bring you to the **Sky Theater** for sky shows with dazzling special effects shown throughout the day.

There is a cafeteria and gift shop in the Planetarium. Admission charge. Skyshow extra. Summer hours: Saturday to Wednesday 9am–6pm, Thursday and Friday 9am–9pm. The rest of the year: Monday to Thursday 9am–5pm, Friday 9am–9pm, Saturday, Sunday, and Holidays 9am–6pm. Free Tuesday. Closed Thanksgiving and Christmas.

4. North Loop

Visit government buildings, outdoor sculptures, and the Chicago Cultural Center. *See map on pages 18–19.*

The three main government buildings in Chicago touch the corner of Clark and Randolph in the Loop. Walk a half block south to start at the **Richard J. Daley Center**, which faces south on Washington Street. The Daley Center houses 31 floors of courtrooms and offices, in a building made of Cor-ten steel. In 1967 an untitled sculpture referred to simply as **The Picasso** was erected in the plaza (*see page 53*). The design was a gift to the city of Chicago from the sculptor himself. It is 50ft (15m) high, and also made of Cor-ten steel. Chicagoans were looking for something more traditional, and 30 years later it still stirs up controversy. There's much disagreement about what it represents. Although the general consensus is that it's a woman, some say it's a bird, others that it's clearly a dog. Picasso never told, so we can only speculate. Only the local kids have no problem with it – they sensibly came to the conclusion years ago that it was a playground climbing frame and as a consequence have endless hours of fun sliding down it. This plaza is also the site of another extraordinary sight – the city's Christmas tree during the holidays. On weekdays enjoy a concert program in the plaza at noon. **Joan Miró's** concrete and mosaic **Chicago sculpture** is across from Daley Center at 69 W. Washington.

Cross Clark Street west of the Daley Center to reach the **City Hall Cook County Building**. The building was designed by Holabird and Roche in 1911 with spacious halls and high ceilings. This is where you will find the Mayor's Office and City Council Chambers. City Council meetings, which are open to the public, are known to generate enough hot air to heat a sauna. If you're interested in attending one, tel: 744-3081 for information on meeting times.

Just north of the County Building across Randolph Street is the **James R. Thompson Center**, the State of Illinois Building, housing state agencies, plus restaurants and shops. You can't miss this striking steel and glass building, designed by Helmut Jahn, which opened in 1985. Go inside to see the interior atrium, and take a stomach-churning ride in glass-enclosed elevators. The Illinois Artisans Shop and the Illinois Art Gallery are worth a visit. The large **fiberglass sculpture** called **Beast** is by artist **Jean Dubuffet**.

If you're hungry, head to **Mac Kelly's Deli**, a block west of the Thompson Center, at the cor-

James R. Thompson Center

Miró's sculpture

Marc Chagall's 'Four Seasons'

ner of Wells and Lake (under the El tracks). You can create your own sandwich or salad and take it to join the lunch crowds for the entertainment in the Daley Center or Thompson Center plazas. Or head a couple blocks south down Clark Street to the **First National Bank Plaza** on Monroe Street. This plaza has a fountain and steps making it a popular spot for office workers to eat a bag lunch. On the Dearborn Street side (east) is **Marc Chagall's Four Seasons** depicting six scenes using stone and glass fragments.

Walk north on Dearborn Street back to Washington Street (Daley Center). Between Daley Center on the west and Marshall Field's on the east is an area called **Block 37**. In summer, it is the site of an outdoor art gallery, **Gallery 37**. In winter it is the site of **Skate on State**, a popular spot for free ice skating, skate rentals available. Chicagoans are a hardy bunch. The temperature might plummet to minus 80 with the wind chill but they'll be out there, skating or jogging. There has been talk that this block is being considered for development, but they'll just find somewhere else.

Continue east on Washington to the **Chicago Cultural Center**, 78 East Washington (between Wabash & Michigan). The Cultural Center features daily programs and exhibits, covering the performing, visual and literary arts. Attend free public events and programs presented by the City of Chicago. For a weekly listing of events, tel: F-I-N-E-A-R-T (346-3278). There is a Chicago Office of Tourism **Visitor Information Center** in the Cultural Center. Watch the 7-minute video *Round the Loop*. A nice touch – the Cultural Center hosts a birthday party every day at 1pm, and everyone is invited, with special treats if it is actually your birthday.

Take the winding staircase to the impressive Preston Bradley Hall on the third floor to see the world's largest stained-glass **Tiffany dome**. Or take an architectural tour of the landmark building offered every Tuesday and Wednesday at 1.30pm, Saturday at 2pm. For tour information call 744-6630.

The **Museum of Broadcast Communications**, tel: 629-6000, in the Cultural Center, showcases the history of television and radio. Visit their TV studio where you can make a tape of yourself as a news anchor, or listen to old TV and radio shows. Open Monday to Saturday 10am–4.30pm, Sunday noon–5pm, closed holidays.

5. Museum of Science and Industry/Hyde Park

Spend as much time as you can at this popular museum which attracts visitors from around the world. Then stroll through Hyde Park and the University of Chicago campus.

The **Museum of Science and Industry**, tel: 773- 684-1414, 57th Street and Lake Shore Drive, appeals to all ages, and is at the eastern end of the Hyde Park neighborhood. There is plenty of parking if you have a car; it's also accessible by CTA or Metra.

Originally constructed as part of the 1839 Columbian Exposition, the building opened as the Museum of Science and Industry in 1933. Julius Rosenwald, Chairman of Sears, donated $7.5 million to refurbish the building in the 1920s. The museum hosts over 2 million visitors a year.

You can spend anywhere from a few hours to an entire day at the museum. There are 75 exhibit halls with over 2000 exhibits. This museum has always been one of my favorite places to visit. It is very heavy on visitor participation, making it a hit with the kids, too. The model railroad takes up a whole room – nothing like you have in your basement. See a fairy castle of miniatures, Yesterday's Main Street – a re-created street from the early 1900s – and Curiosity Place for young children. The coal mine has been completely refurbished (insofar as you can refurbish a coalmine); enter an elevator which lowers you into the mine where you can see what it's like to work hundreds of feet below the surface. Walk through a U-505 German submarine captured during WW II. On the balcony level, learn about the human body; walk through The Heart, a 16-foot pulsating model; and experiment with computers.

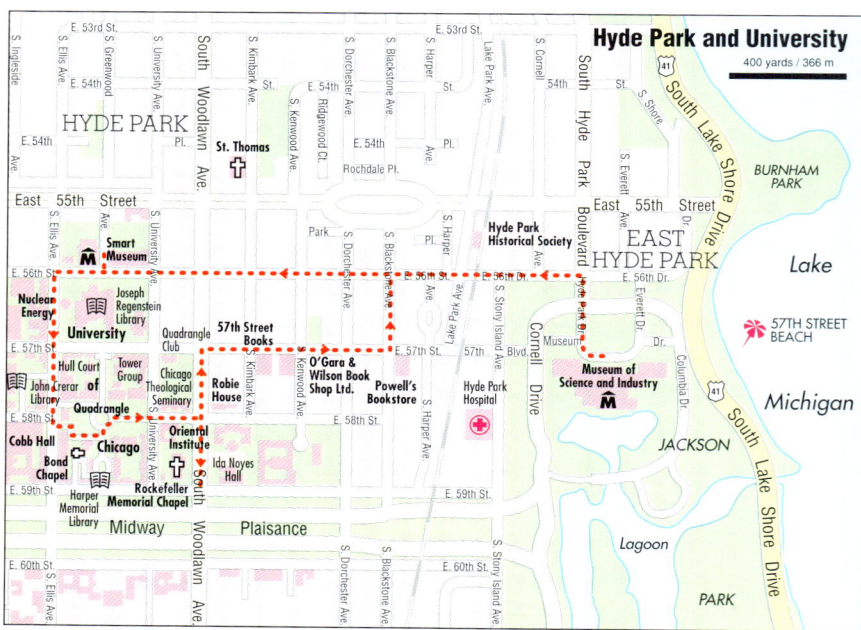

Museum of Science and Industry

Watch baby chicks peck their way out of their shells. Step inside the Whispering Gallery – you'll find you can hear better than you thought. Let the kids have a go, too.

Henry Crown Space Center chronicles our explorations of outer space with spaceships, lunar models and moon rocks. This is where you'll find the **Omnimax Theater**, with a 76-inch (2m) wide five-story tall screen. Purchase tickets upon arrival at the museum (or make reservations). A well-known special event is *Christmas Around the World*, when trees are decorated in the traditional style of various countries. You might also want to visit the gift shop where science toys, books, and T-shirts are sold.

Admission charge. Children under half price. Theater extra. Free Thursday (pay for theater only). Hours: Memorial Day to Labor Day, daily 9.30am–5.30pm; off season, Monday to Friday 9.30am–4pm, Saturday, Sunday and holidays: 9.30am–5.30pm. Closed Christmas.

University of Chicago

If you have time after visiting the museum, explore the **Hyde Park** neighborhood directly west of the museum (but not after dark). Hyde Park is home to the **University of Chicago (U of C)**, which was opened in 1892, and was modeled after England's Oxford University. The opening of the U of C was one of two events largely responsible for the development of Hyde Park. The other was the Columbian Exposition of 1893. The Museum of Science and Industry building was built for the Expo, as was the **Midway Plaisance** which runs between 59th and 60th streets. Feel free to wander the neighborhood, but I'll give you a route to help you find a few of the highlights.

Exit the Museum of Science and Industry, and turn left (west) on 56th Street. You might like to start or end your walk at **Piccolo Mondo**, tel: 643-1106, 1642 East 56th Street, a friendly, relaxed Italian cafe that's a favorite haunt of professors and doctors from the university. Sit at a window table with a view of Hyde Park and enjoy a meal. The food is fresh and good.

Walk west on 56th Street to Greenwood Avenue, turn right to the **Smart Museum**, 5550 South Greenwood Avenue, where the fine arts holdings of the university are displayed. This collection of more than 7,000 objects includes sculptures, photographs, and furniture, as well as paintings. Admission is free, or just see the adjacent sculpture garden. Return to 56th Street, and walk a block further west to Ellis. Turn left (south). On your left about half a block down is a 3-ton bronze sculpture by the British artist, **Henry Moore**, titled **Nuclear Energy**. It commemorates the first nuclear chain reaction achieved below ground (approximately where the sculpture stands, under the bleachers of what was then Stagg Field), by Enrico Fermie and other scientists on December 2, 1942.

Cross 57th Street, and continue south to **Cobb Hall**, the home of the **Renaissance Society**. The society was founded in 1915 to identify living artists whose work would have a lasting influence. See what the art and artists of the future may be. Take the small passageway just north of Cobb Hall to enter the university quadrangle. Cross the quadrangle, and exit onto University Avenue. Just east of University Avenue on 58th Street you'll find the **Oriental Institute,** containing a major collection of art, religious articles, and everyday objects from the ancient Near East. The Institute offers free admission, and is closed on Monday.

From here you can go directly to **Robie House** by taking a right on 58th Street, then turn left at the corner onto Woodlawn Avenue. If you would like to see the Midway Plaisance, go one block south on University Avenue to 59th Street. The strip of land straight ahead is the Midway Plaisance, which was created to replicate a Venetian canal for the Expo.

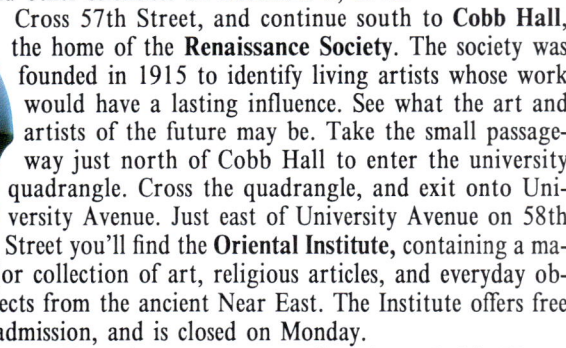

'Nuclear Energy'

However, when it was filled with water, houses throughout the area flooded, and the plan was abandoned. To your left is **Rockefeller Memorial Chapel**, 5850 Woodlawn, named in honor of the founder of the University, John D. Rockefeller. Go north on Woodlawn about a block to Robie House, tel: 702-8374, 5757 Woodlawn. Robie House is Frank Lloyd Wright's 1909 architectural masterpiece, which many consider the culmination of his visionary architecture innovations. Free tours offered at noon.

As you walk east on 57th Street, you'll pass three bookstores. The first is **57th Street Books**, tel: 684-1300, 1301 East 57th Street,

Robie House

which carries current books of general interest and a large children's section. **O'Gara & Wilson Book Shop Ltd**, tel: 363-0993, 1311 East 57th Street, offers a great selection of used books. Just past Blackstone Avenue is **Powell's Bookstore**, 955-7780, 1501 East 57th Street, with another large selection of used books. Go north on Blackstone to 56th Street, turn right, and continue east back to Piccolo Mondo or the Museum of Science and Industry.

6. Architecture Tours

Take a tour of noteworthy Chicago architecture with a highly knowledgeable guide.

The Chicago Architecture Foundation, tel: 922-TOUR (8687), 224 South Michigan Avenue (Santa Fe Building), or 875 North Michigan Avenue (John Hancock Center), for recorded tour information, is dedicated to advancing public interest and education in Chicago's outstanding architectural legacy through a program of tours, exhibits, lectures and special events. The foundation offers a variety of walking, bus or boat tours. Call for details and to make a reservation if needed. Or request a Chicago Architecture Tours brochure, which will tell you times of tours, costs, and duration of the individual tours. A large variety of outings are offered including tours of historic houses or buildings, as well as neighborhoods, hotels, Graceland Cemetery, bike tours of Lincoln Park or the lakefront, a Lunchtime Loop Walking Tour, River Cruise, and Streeterville.

Group tours can be arranged for parties of 10 or more with at least six weeks' notice by calling the Chicago Architecture Foundation Tour Coordinator at tel: 922-3432, extension 226. Foundation hours are Monday to Saturday 9am–7pm, Sunday hours tend to vary, so call ahead to inquire.

Graceland Cemetery

7. Blues Clubs

Visit a number of well-known clubs on the North Side or the South Side devoted almost exclusively to the blues.

The early blues from the Mississippi delta usually meant one man with an acoustic guitar. Chicago blues more likely feature an electric guitar and an entire band. This is the sound that had such an influence on rock music. Chicago's love affair with the blues stretches back to the 1940s when singer and guitarist Muddy Waters is credited with bringing the sound to Chicago. As blacks from the South came up the Mississippi River to Chicago in search of jobs following World War II, they settled primarily on the south and the west sides of the city. The Southern musicians followed their audience to Chicago. During the 1950s, names like Muddy Waters, Howlin Wolf, Otis Rush and Little Walter ruled the Chicago blues scene with their amplified sounds. Many of the performers recorded for Chess Records, including Chicago's legendary Buddy Guy. Women, such as Chicago's Queen of Blues Koko Taylor, were also able to perform the blues. Today, the blues clubs that originated on the south and west sides have shifted to downtown and the north side. Hear some of the old names from the 1950s and 1960s, as well as up-and-coming artists, both local and national, men and women, at the many clubs in Chicago devoted to this musical form.

For non-stop blues music, try to time your trip for the beginning of June to catch Chicago's **Blues Fest** at Grant Park and join the festive atmosphere under the stars. Bring a blanket, pack a picnic, and get into the fun as blues performers from around the country gather for three days of live performances.

If you can't make the festival, you can still hear the blues in Chicago any night of the year. Depending on where you are, how much traveling you want to do, and whether you want to spend your time at one club or plan to bar-hop, there's plenty to choose from. There are two clusters of clubs in Chicago, in River North and Lincoln Park, ideal for pub-crawlers. There's also one club on the south side of the Loop well worth a visit. And although it's far from the downtown area, true blues fans will appreciate a visit to a South Side neighborhood club. What can you expect from a blues club? The atmosphere is dark and smoky, the emphasis is on the music, casual dress is the norm. Some clubs serve food, but many only offer a bar. Some have a dance floor. Doors generally open at 8pm, with music starting around 9pm. Earliest closing is 2am, and some stay open till 5am on Saturday. Minimum entry age is 21. Cover charge is usual.

Blue Chicago

To start at a central location, pick one of the River North clubs. **Blue Chicago**, tel: 642-6261, 736 North Clark (between Superior and Chicago), and **Blue Chicago on Clark**, tel: 661-0100, 536 N. Clark (between Grand and Ohio), only two blocks south, are both a few blocks west of the North Michigan Avenue hotels.

Blue Chicago on Clark is located in a former speakeasy. Both clubs have the same owner, and one cover charge will get you into both clubs. Both also have dance floors and serve drinks only. There's live music nightly (though each is closed one night of the week), and female performers often appear.

If you plan to be in Lincoln Park, or if you'd like to visit as many blues clubs as possible, take a cab about 2 miles north to the Lincoln Park neighborhood where you'll find three clubs in walking distance of each other.

Kingston Mines, tel: 773-477-4646, 2548 North Halsted, is the North Side's oldest and biggest club. It's also the only one with two stages providing continuous music and you're free to move from one to the other. There are dance floors in front of both stages and food is served. Performers are primarily local with bigger names on the weekend. Less than a block south is **B.L.U.E.S.**, tel: 773-528-1012, 2519 North Halsted, a small, funky, friendly club that books top local artists and gets very crowded on weekend nights. Come early if you hope to get a seat. Don't come hungry, though – no food is served.

For a different atmosphere walk one block west on Altgeld (the first street south of B.L.U.E.S. on the west side of the street) to Lincoln Avenue. A few doors north is **Lilly's**, tel: 525-2422, 2513 N. Lincoln Avenue, a tiny club with a cozy balcony, featuring primarily local talent. Small dance floor, drinks only served.

If you're staying at the Chicago Hilton or the Blackstone Hotel, or if you just want to go to just one club, make it **Buddy Guy's Legends**, tel: 427-0333, 754 South Wabash, just south of the Loop. Legends attracts fans from around the world and is one of the best blues clubs in the country. Owned by the Grammy Award-winning blues icon Buddy Guy, who's frequently at the club performing and mingling when he happens to be in town, Legends is also visited by bluesmen and rock performers such as Eric Clapton when they're in town.

Thanks to a raised stage you can see and hear the entertainment from anywhere in this big, friendly, crowded place. A large collection of blues memorabilia adorns the walls, including Buddy's many awards. This is a spot to listen to the music so you won't find a dance floor, but the kitchen serves great Louisiana-style soul food.

For serious blues fans, **New Checkerboard Lounge**, tel: 773-624-3240, 423 East 43rd Street, is about as authentic as you can get. Once owned by Buddy Guy, it's the oldest blues club in Chicago, and is considered one of the great old South Side clubs. Anybody who is anybody has played here at some time. The Checkerboard attracts both locals and serious blues fans, but it's about 8 miles south of downtown and not in the best of areas so don't make it an opportunity to explore. A car or cab would be better than public transportation. Live music Wednesday to Saturday.

8. Gangster Tour

So ya wanna see da places where Al Capone took care of business? Hop on da bus, but make sure ya know the password.

An **Untouchables Tour** is a two-hour trip to gangster-era landmarks. Call 773-881-1195 to make a reservation. Take a ride in an old school bus with windows riddled with (fake) bullet holes. The tour is led by two energetic pinstriped "gangsters" telling you about their buddies through historically correct gangster facts. This entertainment on wheels tour will visit the places where **Al Capone** did business, taking you past the site of the flower store near Holy Name Cathedral where Dion O'Banion took a fatal bullet barrage, and Holy Name Cathedral where Earl Hymie Weisse was gunned down, not forgetting the Biograph Theater where the Lady in Red betrayed John Dillinger. Admission charge heftier than most attractions, but it's very entertaining and worth it if gangster lore interests you. There are tours Monday to Saturday at 10am, Thursday to Saturday at 1pm, Friday at 7.30pm, Saturday at 5pm, Sunday at 11am and 2pm. Reservations are suggested using MasterCard or Visa. The tours

The long arm of the law

The Bulls champion scores again

leave from Clark and Ohio (in front of Rock-N-Roll McDonald's). Packages are available for private groups of 15 or more, which can include dinner reservations at Tommy Gun's (*see below*). Note that most of the sites are no longer used as they were at the time of Al Capone, but the tour is a lot of fun and does provide historically accurate information.

After the tour, there are a number of fun restaurants in the area. You will be let off back at **Rock-N-Roll McDonald's** ($), tel: 664-7940, 600 N Clark, which offers the standard McDonald's menu. Decor includes rock 'n' roll memorabilia, a 1959 Corvette in the dining room, and life-size Beatles statues positioned like the *Abbey Road* album cover. See Elvis, Mickey Mouse, Howdy Doody, Frankie Avalon, Little Richard – everything the baby-boomers grew up with. Booths have mini juke boxes. It's worth a look even if you don't plan to eat here. Nearby, the **Hard Rock Cafe** ($$), tel: 943-2252, 63 West Ontario, is a typical branch of the chain. Again the theme is rock 'n' roll. **Michael Jordan's Restaurant** ($$$), tel: 644-3865, 500 North LaSalle, is also close by. You might have guessed this restaurant has a sports theme. This is the basketball star's restaurant, emphasizing his favorite food and sport.

If you're in the mood to continue with the gangster theme, consider **Tommy Gun's Garage** ($$$), tel: 773-RAT-A-TAT (728-2828), 1239 S State (Roosevelt and State). Visit this speakeasy, featuring dinner and a show with singing, dancing, comedy, and audience participation. Free attendant parking. Enter in the rear (where else would you enter a speakeasy?) under the El tracks where you'll be greeted by a man called Gloves. Look out – he has a tommy gun. Know the password. Watch silent movies while you eat. About an hour and a half later, when everyone has finished dinner, the musical comedy revue starts, so plan to spend around 3 hours here. Doors open Thursday and Saturday at 6.30, Friday 7.30 and Sunday at 6 for dinner. Reservations required with a deposit or credit card. Prices include tax and tip. Everything but the hooch.

On a Hard Rock roll

9. Sports Teams

Chicago takes its sports seriously. Depending on the season, choose baseball, basketball, football or hockey.

Baseball

Chicago is a baseball town. We're lucky to have two teams, which creates some friendly competition between Southsiders and Northsiders. You'll find that people are either White Sox fans or Cubs fans – not both. For years, one of the favorite games of the season was the Crosstown Classic, an exhibition game between the two Chicago teams that, although the fans took quite seriously, didn't count in the standings. League rules have changed, and the two teams now play each other as part of their regular season. Unless you're a fan of one of the teams, choose which to see play by the neighborhood you're closer to, how their schedule fits in your plans, or whether you prefer a modern stadium or a cozy ballpark. Baseball season runs from April to early October, and most games are generally played at night.

Southsiders root for the **Chicago White Sox**. The White Sox are part of the American League, playing at **Comiskey Park**, 35th & Dan Ryan Expressway, tel: 924-1000. This new stadium opened on April 19, 1991 and is a very large, modern structure, replacing the oldest stadium in the major league which was right across the street in what is now a parking lot. The highest seats are far from the action and very steep, but do offer a different view of the game (although you might want to bring binoculars if you choose these seats). Sometimes fellow fans provide the entertainment – one recent visitor was riveted by the yelling, cheering and general enthusiasm of the four nuns perched in front of her. Fireworks are set off for each home run hit by the Sox. To reach Comiskey Park, take an A or B Dan Ryan El Train to 35th Street and you'll see the stadium just to the west of the El. Get tickets in advance by phone or on game day at the box office. The Stadium is so big that sold-out games are not usually a problem. The food here is surprisingly good, by the way.

Where fans have a ball

The **Chicago Cubs**, who play in the National League, are the Northside team. They play at **Wrigley Field**, 1060 W. Addison Street (Addison and Clark) tel: 773-404-2827. Wrigley Field is best recognized by its ivy-covered walls. After much resistance, lights were finally installed in the ballpark in 1988 so night games could be played, but the Cubs still play many games in the afternoon. Join the Bleacher Bums in the outfield bleachers and sing *Take Me Out To The Ballgame* with sportscaster Harry Caray during the seventh-inning stretch. Although the last time the Cubs played in a World Series was in 1945, true fans are always confident that this will be the year for their beloved Cubbies. To reach Wrigley Field take the Howard Street El line to Addison. For ticket information, call tel: 773-404-CUBS (2827); outside Illinois, call tel: 800-347-CUBS (2827). Cubs fans like to linger in the neighborhood after games, so join other fans at the Cubby Bear across the street or in another nearby bar to celebrate the game – win or lose.

Football

The **Chicago Bears** have been playing in **Soldier Field** near the lake at McFetridge Drive & Lake Shore Drive, tel: 294-2200, just south of the Field Museum, since 1971. Football season runs from September to December. Subscription sales usually account for all tickets, but call to inquire at tel: 847-615-2327. Another possible ticket source is a ticket broker. They charge a premium, but it may be the only way to get tickets to some of the sold-out games. A tradition that fans seem to enjoy as much as the games is the pre-game tailgate parties they hold by their cars in the parking lot before heading in to the open-air stadium to watch the Monsters of the Midway clash with another National Football League team.

Basketball and Hockey

Two teams share the **United Center**, 1901 West Madison, tel: 445-4500. Built in 1994 across the street from the old Chicago Stadium, which has since been torn down, the United Center is a very modern facility with comfortable seats, plush suites (the old stadium had no skyboxes), plenty of restrooms and concession stands. It also boasts an eight-sided color video scoreboard that weighs 50,000 pounds, is said to have cost $6 million, and can be as much fun to watch as the game itself. There's seating for over 20,000 fans, yet basketball games are still often sold out.

The Bulls and the beers

The United Center is the place to see the five-time World Champion **Chicago Bulls** play basketball, during the season that runs from November to May. This is where basketball supremo Michael Jordan returned to the game in March of 1995 after taking a year off to play baseball. His number 23 jersey was taken out of retirement, and the team continued to dominate basketball in the 1990s, winning their fifth NBA championship in 1997. There's even a life-size bronze statue of Michael Jordan outside the United Center, probably the only way to get a picture with him these days.

When the Bulls aren't playing, the United Center is transformed into an ice arena for the **Chicago Blackhawks**, Chicago's hockey team. In spite of talented individual players, this team has gone longer than any other without winning a championship, yet they still have a huge following. Chicagoans are not fair weather fans.

10. River North

Visit this exciting new neighborhood and soak up the art gallery atmosphere. Or perhaps even buy a painting.

Approximate River North boundaries are Chicago Avenue on the North, the Chicago River on the south, Orleans Street on the west, and Dearborn Street on the east. The area was a former industrial and warehouse district which had fallen into disrepair before artists began moving here, attracted by the spacious buildings and low rents. Renovation began, and now you'll find rehabbed loft buildings occupied by auction houses, antique dealers, and jewelers. Many of the hottest new restaurants and clubs are opening here. Art galleries are thick on the ground. River North has the greatest concentration of galleries in Chicago, as a matter of fact the largest concentration outside of Manhattan. The majority are located within a block or two of Superior and Franklin Streets, an area sometimes referred to as **SuHu** (for Superior and Huron), making a word play on New York's SoHo art district.

Here's a sampling of galleries, and the type of work they carry. Starting at 325 West Huron, Zolla/Lieberman specializes in contemporary painting, sculpture, drawing and photography. Heading east, Nicole Gallery, 230 Huron, features works by Haitian artists and ethnic art. Turn north at Wells to Gwenda Jay Gallery, 704 Wells, for American and European artists. Then turn west on Superior to Ann Nathan Gallery, 218 Superior, for paintings by contemporary artists, sculpture and furniture. At 230 Superior you'll find Marx-Saunders Gallery, Ltd. with studio glass art sculpture, and the Schneider Gallery featuring photography and jewelry. Turn north onto Franklin to reach Mary Bell Galleries, 740 Franklin, for American contemporary art, old master works and picture framing. Nine galleries in less than 5 blocks, and just a fraction of the total.

Merchandise Mart

So, wander, browse, enjoy. Most galleries are open weekdays and Saturday 10am or 11am–5pm, some open earlier, some stay open later, but if you plan on these hours, you'll be playing it safe. Openings of new exhibits usually take place on Friday evenings, 5pm–8pm. The public is invited and welcome. Refreshments are usually served, and artists are frequently present. Pick up a copy of the *Chicago Gallery News* at the Pumping Station or your hotel (or write to request a copy from 107 West Delaware Place, 60610) for more information on the galleries.

In August, River North hosts the **Gold Coast Art Fair**, the largest art fair in the world. It takes place on the sidewalks around the intersection of Erie and Wells streets. Some 400 artists from around the country display and sell their work. There's no charge to attend. Tel: 787-2677 for information.

Merchandise Mart, tel: 527-7600, on the river between Orleans and Wells streets, contains more square feet than any other building in the country except the Pentagon. Built by the architectural firm of Graham Anderson Probst and White in 1930, it's now owned by the Kennedys. Showrooms are open for tours only (weekdays at noon). Two floors of retail stores are for good shopping.

When you're ready to eat, there's a lot to choose from. **Carsons The Place for Ribs** ($$$), tel: 289-9200, 312 N. Wells Street, offers good ribs and other American fare; **Centro** ($$), tel: 988-7775, 710 North Wells Street, has good Italian dishes, as does **Lino's** ($$$) (*see Eating Out*).

11. Oprah Winfrey Show

Visit the taping of a TV talk show. Here's your chance to appear on television, but plan this at least a month in advance.

Did you hear what Oprah said today? Is a last name really necessary? Since its syndicated debut in 1986, **The Oprah Winfrey Show** has remained the number one talk show in television history, seen by 15 to 20 million viewers a day in the United States, as well as internationally. Oprah first came to Chicago in 1984 to host WLS-TVs *AM Chicago*. With the success she brought to the show, it was expanded to an hour and renamed *The Oprah Winfrey Show*. When Harpo (Oprah spelled backwards) Production Co. took over ownership and production responsibilities in 1988, Oprah, clearly an astute businesswoman, became the first woman to own and produce her own television talk show.

Oprah has a dedicated following. She knows how to connect with an audience. She's also influential way beyond the scope of the show, and this in-

Talk show queen Oprah

fluence was never more apparent than when she introduced a new segment on her show called Oprah's Book Club. Now, book authors and publishers have joined the legions of Oprah fans, for any book appearing on her show is guaranteed to shoot to the top of the best-selling list. When Oprah told her audience to read *The Deep End of the Ocean*, Jacquelyn Mitchard's first novel, for example, it rose to the top of the *New York Times'* fiction best-seller list. Sales of *Song of Solomon* by Toni Morrison, first published in 1977, rose from a steady 50,000 copies a year to a staggering 500,000. Bookstores and libraries are enthused about Winfrey's efforts to promote reading, but can't keep up with the demand because when Oprah tells her audience to read a particular book, they do.

The best place to see this very influential Chicago celebrity up close is at **Harpo Studios**, 110 N. Carpenter, on the Near West Side, at a taping of her show. Join about 200 other people in the audience. From the warm-up by the audience coordinator to the bright lights of the TV studio to the first glimpse of Oprah, and the chance to see her in real life, it's an hour that Oprah adorers will remember for a long time. There's the excitement of being part of a real TV show, knowing the right reaction will catch the cameraman's attention and get you on TV, or the right question or comment might be used on the show. Not to mention the opportunity to shake hands with Oprah after the taping.

The show is taped in Chicago on Tuesday, Wednesday, and Thursday at 9am and noon. There is no charge to be in the audience, but you must have a reservation, which they recommend be made at least a month in advance. The show currently takes reservations only by phone; mail and e-mail requests aren't accepted. Tel: 591-9222 but be prepared to take some time to get through on the reservation line. Limit of four tickets, which are available only to adults.

There are two other talk shows taped in Chicago which also accept reservations for their audience. **Jerry Springer**, tel: 321-5350, or **Jenny Jones**, tel: 836-9400 are both taped at NBC Tower, 454 North Columbus Drive. If coming from Michigan Avenue, you can walk along the upper north bank of the Chicago River to reach **NBC Tower**. As with Oprah, it's best to make reservations about a month ahead of time.

None of the shows can tell you the topic of the show you will be attending when you make your reservation. You just have to take your chance for an opportunity to be on television and part of the fun.

An invitation from Oprah?

Eating Out

Now comes the biggest challenge of your vacation – choosing where to eat. Chicago has an abundance of restaurants. When asked for a few favorites, one Chicago resident listed 98! Chicago has everything from fine dining to neighborhood bars where they'll throw a burger on the grill for you. Ethnic restaurants abound. You can get good Chinese food downtown, although some insist you have to go to Chinatown; same with Greek dishes. Italian restaurants are very popular right now, but it's a completely different experience in Little Italy itself. Then of course there's pizza, glorious pizza, or more specifically deep dish pizza, an original Chicago dish. I've included both downtown and neighborhood choices for you wherever possible.

For a sampling from many restaurants, check out the Taste of Chicago, a lakefront festival featuring over 50 different Chicago restaurants held in late June and early July. Expect a crowd; but since it's held outdoors in Grant Park, there's room for everyone. In addition to food, there's music and entertainment and it's lots of fun.

Always call ahead to see if you need a restaurant reservation. At some of the more expensive restaurants, reservations must be made weeks in advance, but for most you can call a day or two ahead, or even the same day. Some will not require or even accept reservations. An approximate price guideline per person, is as follows: $ = under $20; $$ = $20-$30; $$$ = $30-$45; $$$$ = over $45.

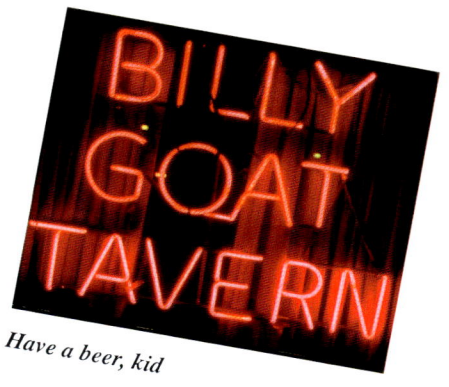

Have a beer, kid

American

BILLY GOAT TAVERN
430 North Michigan Avenue
(lower level)
Tel: 222-1525
This is not a great restaurant and it's in an odd location under Michigan Avenue, but it was immortalized in the *Saturday Night Live* skits with the late John Belushi. So come order a 'cheeseborger...cheeseborger' and a 'Pepsi – no Coke'. It's a favorite hangout of reporters. $

BUB CITY CRABSHACK
901 North Weed Street
Tel: 266-1200
Southern style crabshack for crabs, barbecue ribs, and fun in a trendy Northside area. $$

HOUSTONS
616 North Rush Street
Tel: 649-1121
Offers a wide range of food to accommodate most palates from fish or ribs, to soup and salad, to steaks or the ubiquitous burger. $$

Chinese

HOUSE OF HUNAN
535 North Michigan Avenue
Tel: 329-9494
Gourmet Chinese, not in Chinatown, but on the Mag Mile. From hot and spicy to mild. $$–$$$

THREE HAPPINESS RESTAURANT
209 West Cermak Road
Tel: 842-1964
Located in Chinatown. Famous for its Dim Sum, specializing in Cantonese/Szechwan cuisine. $

French

CHARLIE TROTTER'S
816 West Armitage
Tel: 773-248-6228
Owner Charlie Trotter is one of the most recognized chefs in the nation. Very expensive award-winning restaurant serving French cuisine with an innovative approach. $$$$

EVEREST
440 South LaSalle
Tel: 663-8920
World renowned chef/owner Jean Joho oversees this very expensive 5-star restaurant serving elegant French cuisine. A spectacular view on the 40th floor of the Chicago Stock Exchange. $$$$

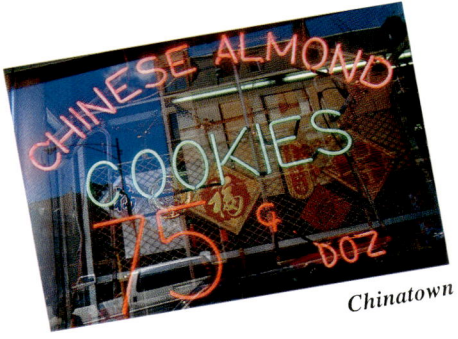

Chinatown

Greek

GREEK ISLANDS
200 South Halsted Street
Tel: 782-9855
A long-time Greektown favorite featuring an exposed steam table. A fun place to eat. $$

PAPAGUS GREEK TAVERNA
600 North State Street
Tel: 642-8550
Enjoy a large selection of appetizers. Specialties include oven-roasted Greek chicken and broiled white fish. $$

Italian

ADAGIO
923 West Weed Street
Tel: 787-0400
Choose the dining room or outdoor garden in this trendy Northside area. Features music on weekends. $$$

AVANZARE
161 East Huron Street
Tel: 337-8056
Good regional Italian cuisine and homemade pasta, just a block off Michigan Avenue. Order from the daily specials list. $$$

BICE RISTORANTE
158 East Ontario Street
Tel: 664-1474
Pastas with innovative sauces. $$$

COCO PAZZO
300 West Hubbard

Tel: 836-0900
Authentic regional Italian cuisine featuring pasta, meat and fish specials. Extensive wine list. Leave room for dessert. $$$

HARRY CARAY'S RESTAURANT
33 West Kinzie Street
Tel: 828-0966
Owned by the famed Cubs sports announcer, who really does stop by, this Italian restaurant is decorated with baseball memorabilia. $$-$$$

LINO'S
222 West Ontario
Tel: 787-5000
Northern Italian food prepared by chefs from Italy. Enjoy homemade pasta and great steaks in River North in a club-like setting. $$$

MAGGIANO'S LITTLE ITALY
516 North Clark Street
Tel: 644-7700
Very good hearty servings in a setting reminiscent of a New York Little Italy dinner house. $$-$$$

THE ROSEBUD CAFE
1500 West Taylor Street
Tel: 942-1117
Quaint Italian restaurant in Little Italy serving great pasta for over 20 years. $$

TUSCANY
1014 West Taylor Street
Tel: 829-1990
At this Tuscan eatery in Little Italy you'll get hearty flavors and simple preparation. Fresh pasta made daily. Try the rotisserie grilled chicken. $$

Mexican

FRONTERA GRILL
455 North Clark Street
Tel: 661-1434
Renowned cafe offering a wonderful variety of regional Mexican cuisine by a chef/owner who wrote *Authentic Mexican*. Try something from the weekly menu. $$

Seafood

CAPE COD ROOM
140 East Walton, in the Drake Hotel
Tel: 787-2200
Enjoy the ambiance of this well-known restaurant with nautical decor. Serving seafood since 1933. $$$$

CATCH 35
35 West Wacker
Tel: 346-3500
35 different fresh seafood dishes featured daily in this beautifully decorated dining room. Piano bar. $$$

NICK'S FISHMARKET
1 First Chicago Plaza
Tel: 621-0200
Delicious seafood in a great atmosphere right downtown. Piano bar. $$$$

SHAW'S CRAB HOUSE
21 East Hubbard Street
Tel: 527-2722
Two restaurants in one located near the River and Michigan Avenue. The lounge is a raw oyster bar; the dining room resembles an old New England seafood house. $$-$$$

Steak

GENE & GEORGETTI
500 North Franklin
Tel: 527-3718
Terrific prime aged steak & Italian specialties have been served in this steakhouse for 55 years. A favorite in our house. $$$

Steak your claim

Eating on the run

GIBSON'S STEAKHOUSE
1028 North Rush Street
Tel: 266-8999
Great old-fashioned steakhouse serving super-sized steaks for super-sized appetites. Piano bar. $$$

Pizza

In addition to Pizzeria Uno or Pizzeria Due, visited on Day 2, try one of the following:

BACINO'S
75 East Wacker Drive
Tel: 263-0070
Very good deep dish pizza. Their specialty is spinach pizza. $

THE ORIGINAL GINO'S EAST (GINO'S)
160 East Superior Street
Tel: 943-1124
Great deep dish pizza. Also thin crust and sandwiches. $

LOU MALNATI'S
439 North Wells Street
Tel: 828-9800
Enjoy deep dish pizza in their sports memorabilia-filled restaurant. They will deliver to hotels. $

Nightlife

No matter what your tastes, you'll have no trouble finding something to do when Chicago comes alive at night. Attend a concert or the ballet. If you're in the mood to see a play, choose from musicals, Shakespeare, audience participation, comedy or mystery. Decide if you want to see local talent or a Broadway show.

Find a quiet piano bar and enjoy the music, or pick a spot to dance to the beat of the band. Or have an uproarious evening at one of the generally excellent comedy clubs. Most of the big hotels have good bars with some type of live entertainment. Chicago is well known for its blues and jazz, and has plenty of clubs featuring both.

Only New York can boast a bigger theater scene than Chicago. Some of the main theaters are listed here, but that's just a start. For comprehensive listings of performances and events, check the *Reader*, or the Friday section of the *Tribune* or *Sun-Times*. Also check the Arts & Entertainment section of the Sunday *Tribune* for theater listings including smaller or less known theaters that might not be included here.

You can also pick up Chicago's *Official Visitors Guide* or the *Chicago Theatre Guide* from the Visitors Center for a complete listing of the current performances.

Tickets for most fine art events are available through Ticketmaster, tel: 902-1500, as well as at the box office. Hot Tix, 977-1755, sells half price tickets (plus service charge) in person on the day of a performance when tickets are available (cash or charge). The two downtown locations are 108 North State Street (across from Marshall Field's department store) and the Historic Water Tower Place at 806 North Michigan Avenue (located at Chicago and Michigan). Hot Tix is also an outlet for all Ticketmaster events (cash only accepted).

Just the ticket

Classical Music

CHICAGO SYMPHONY ORCHESTRA
Orchestra Hall
220 South Michigan Avenue
Tel: 294-3000
In summer:
Ravinia, Highland Park
Tel: 847-728-4642

LYRIC OPERA
20 North Wacker Drive
Tel: 332-2244
Season runs September to February.

GRANT PARK SYMPHONY ORCHESTRA AND CHORUS
Petrillo Music Shell in Grant Park
Tel: 742-4763 for concert hotline
Free outdoor concerts through the Chicago Park District. Call for schedule which also includes guest artists.

Dance

BALLET CHICAGO
Tel: 993-7575
Classical ballet troupe.

HUBBARD STREET DANCE
Tel: 663-0853
Contemporary dance set to contemporary music.

Theater

ARIE CROWN THEATRE
McCormick Place
2300 South Lake Shore Drive
Tel: 791-6000

AUDITORIUM THEATRE
50 East Congress Parkway
Tel: 902-1500
National landmark building, featuring touring productions.

GOODMAN THEATRE
200 South Columbus Drive
Tel: 443-3800
Performances using different casts for different shows.

Auditorium Theatre

MAYFAIR THEATRE
Blackstone Hotel
636 South Michigan Avenue
Tel: 786-9120
Shear Madness has been playing since 1982.

SHUBERT THEATRE
22 West Monroe Street
Tel: 977-1700
Touring productions.

STEPPENWOLF THEATRE COMPANY
1650 North Halsted Street
Tel: 335-1650
Ensemble troupe performing different shows.

Comedy

COMEDY SPORTZ
3209 North Halsted Street
Tel: 773-549-8080
Two teams of comedians compete in improvisational sketches based on audience suggestions with the audience at the end judging the competition.

First-rate comedy

IMPROV OLYMPIC
3541 North Clark Street
Tel: 773-880-0199
Alumni include John Belushi and Chris Farley.

SECOND CITY
1616 N. Wells
Tel: 337-3992
Since 1959 signature brand of social-political satire. Starting point of many famous actors, directors and writers.

SECOND CITY ETC
1608 N Wells
Tel: 642-8189
Companion theater; different shows. Free improvisations after last show (except Friday). Dinner/theater packages available. No drink minimum.

ZANIES COMEDY CLUB
1548 N. Wells
Tel: 337-4027

Professional stand-up comedy club. Past performers have included Jay Leno, Tim Allen and Jerry Seinfeld.

Music

If you've come to town determined to visit Rush Street head to Division between Clark and State streets, where you will find a slew of singles bars. Similar offerings can be found on North Pier, 455 E. Illinois, at Baja Beach Club. If your idea of a night on the town is a wet T-shirt contest, this is the place for you. Don't say I didn't warn you.

Blues

Chicago-style blues began on the South Side. Today's clubs are mostly on the North Side. *See Pick & Mix 7.*

Jazz

ANDY'S JAZZ CLUB
11 East Hubbard Street
Tel: 642-6805
One of Chicago's best spots for serious jazz. Spacious sophisticated saloon atmosphere, casual dining.

THE BOP SHOP
1807 W. Division
Tel: 235-3232
Small local groups play in an intimate setting at this Wicker Park Club.

THE BULLS NIGHTCLUB
1916 N. Lincoln Park W
Tel: 773-337-3000
Small club with intimate atmosphere showcases the best of local groups. Superior acoustics.

THE COTTON CLUB
1710 S. Michigan
Tel: 341-9787
Jazz club committed to a tradition of sophistication, elegance and nostalgia. A favorite of upscale young black professionals. Open mike Monday.

DICK'S LAST RESORT
435 E. Illinois Street (North Pier)
Tel: 836-7870
Crowded raucous North Pier fixture has hot Dixieland jazz most nights of the week. No cover, no dress code and assuredly no class.

GOLD STAR SARDINE BAR
680 N Lake Shore Drive
Tel: 664-4215
Housed in a splendid renovated building, this tiny, aptly-named spot with seating for 60 books top names such as Tony Bennett, Liza Minnelli that attract a trendy clientele.

THE GREEN MILL
4802 N. Broadway
Tel: 773-878-5552
This popular former 1920s speakeasy features local jazz musicians and a hip, funky atmosphere. On Sunday evening check out the Uptown Poetry Slam, a competitive poetry reading that takes center stage.

POPS FOR CHAMPAGNE
2943 N. Sheffield Avenue
773-472-1000
Jazz, champagne, appetizers and desserts. Combination of large outdoor garden and two fireplaces make Pops the perfect gathering place all year round. Also open for Sunday brunch with live jazz.

Rock

CABARET METRO
3730 N. Clark
Tel: 773-549-0203
Wide range of artists from nationally known to local, and a wide range of rock styles.

CUBBY BEAR
1059 W. Addison Street
Tel: 773-327-1662
Variety of acts play this scruffy but roomy venue across the street from Wrigley Field. Music starts around 10pm. During baseball season opens in the afternoon for Cubs fans.

LOUNGE AX
2438 N Lincoln Avenue
Tel: 773-525-6620
Mix of local rock, folk, country and reggae acts presented nightly.

Dance Club

EXCALIBUR
632 N. Dearborn Parkway.
Tel: 266-1944
Chicago's largest nightclub. Four floors offering dancing, live music and DJs, billiard rooms, game emporium and late-nite restaurant for energetic night owls.

Piano

COQ D'OR RESTAURANT AND LOUNGE
Drake Hotel
140 E. Walton Street
Tel: 787-2200
Intimate atmosphere reminiscent of an English pub.

Beat the blues

Shopping

There are two major shopping areas in Chicago, North Michigan Avenue and State Street. For North Michigan Avenue, which features glitzy shops, name-brand shops, famous name-brand apparel, and vertical malls, turn back to Pick & Mix on page 45, where it is already covered in detail.

STATE STREET

State Street, often referred to as that great street, has seen many stores move to North Michigan Avenue, but the anchors of State Street – Wabash Avenue area, Marshall Field's and Carson's – remain in all their elegance. If you're here at Christmas time, children and adults alike will be entranced by Marshall Field's detailed and elaborate window display.

Carson Pirie Scott & Company, 1 South State Street, tel: 641-7000, is a full department store whose association with Chicago shoppers goes back more than 140 years. The Corporate Level offers clothing for executives, as well as a personal wardrobe consultant while InPulse appeals to teenagers. The store occupies a landmark building by architect Louis Sullivan that is considered to be one of his showcases. Note the iron scrollwork in the doorway at the corner of State and Madison streets, which shows Sullivan at his most ornate.

Marshall Field's & Company, 111 N. State Street, tel: 781-1000. A paradise of shopping with over a hundred departments, Marshall Field's flagship store has nine floors and seven restaurants – eating under the Christmas tree in the Walnut Room over the holidays is a Chicago tradition. This is old Chicago and Marshall Field's has been serving customers since the 1850s – the founder's motto was 'Give the lady what she wants!' The store has undergone a major renovation and, other than the atrium with its more modern look, evokes a turn of the century charm. Note the Tiffany glass dome in the southwest atrium, near State

Carson Pirie Scott

and Washington. Field's melt-away Frango mints, produced in their State Street kitchens, make a great edible Chicago souvenir or present and can be shipped world-wide.

Other stores on State Street rubbing shoulders with Marshall Field's and Carson Pirie Scott & Co. include The Body Shop, 3 N. State, for attractive toiletries and lotions; Crate & Barrel, 101 N. Wabash, for decorator housewares; The Gap, 133 N. Wabash, always popular with teenagers and young adults; and Filene's Basement, and T J Maxx, 1 N. State, for bargain name-brand apparel.

OTHER SHOPPING AREAS

Merchandise Mart is just north of the Chicago River between Wells and Orleans streets, tel: 527-4141. Carson Pirie Scott & Company has a branch here, as do a number of well known stores such as The Gap, Crabtree & Evelyn, Lerner New York, and Casual Corner. Although best known for its decorator showrooms, the only way to see the showrooms is with your interior designer or on a tour as they're not open to the public. Shopping Monday to Friday 9am–6pm, Saturday 10am–5pm.

Retail therapy opportunity

Oak Street between Michigan Avenue and Rush Street features the incomparably fashionable Barney's at 25 East Oak, as well as Giorgio Armani at 113 East Oak, Gianni Versace at 101 East Oak, Sonia Rykiel at 106 East Oak, and Ultimo at 114 East Oak. The street for those to whom money is no object; a great window shopping opportunity for the rest of us.

River North is the center for art galleries, furnishing stores and boutiques and there's a high concentration of shops in a small area – the perfect place to do a lot of shopping without a lot of walking. The *Chicago Gallery News* (available at the Tourist Information Center at Water Tower) provides an up-to-date listing of current art gallery exhibits.

North Pier, 435 East Illinois Street, tel: 836-4300, is an 85-year-old rehabbed waterfront warehouse containing specialty shops, restaurants, bars, and a number of activities. There's a Nature Museum Shop connected to the museum and a holography gallery that has holograms in every imaginable form; there are video game rooms and laser games. Liberate your cash and acquire kites, sunglasses, art work, cards, clothing, and souvenirs of Chicago. Rent a bicycle, play pool or miniature golf, have a drink in Baja Beach Club, or listen to Dixie music at Dick's Last Resort.

Well-dressed window on Michigan Avenue

ANTIQUES

There are only a couple of antique dealers in or near downtown:

ANTIQUES ON THE AVENUE
(Across from the Art Institute)
104 South Michigan, Suite 200
Tel: 357-2800
THE ANTIQUES CENTRE AT KINZIE SQUARE
220 West Kinzie Street
Tel: 464-1946

The antique district is on the north side in northern Lincoln Park near Lincoln and Belmont:

Belmont Antique Malls
2039 West Belmont
Tel: 773-549-9270
2229 West Belmont
Tel: 773-871-3915
Chicago Antique Mall
3045 North Lincoln Avenue
Tel: 773-929-0200
Lincoln Antique Mall
3141 North Lincoln Avenue
Wrigleyville Antique Mall
3336 North Clark Street
Tel: 773-868-0285

BOOKS

BARBARA'S BOOKSTORE, Oak Park and Navy Pier. Good range.
PRAIRIE AVENUE BOOKSTORE, 418 South Wabash. Architecture.
BORDERS, 830 North Michigan Avenue. Mega-bookstore.

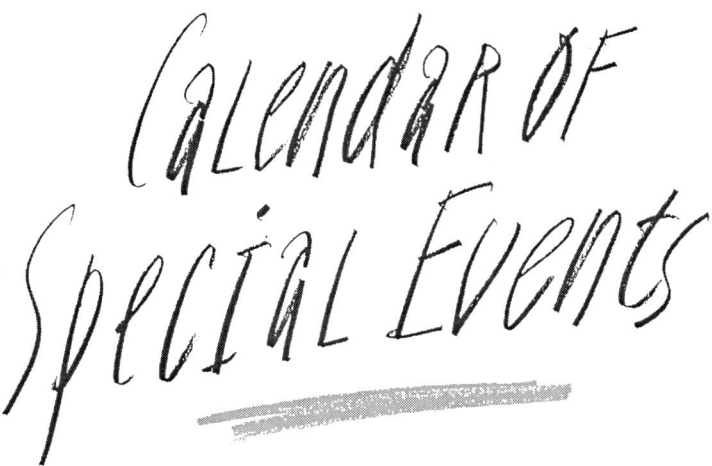

Calendar of Special Events

There's always something going on in Chicago; for precise dates and details, check the *Reader*, a free weekly paper distributed on Thursday, or read the *Friday* section of the *Chicago Tribune* or the *Weekender* section of the *Chicago Sun-Times*, both in the Friday edition of the papers. You can also contact the Chicago Office of Tourism at 1-800-CONNECT to receive a free visitor information packet on events and attractions.

In addition to the annual events listed here, many of the museums and cultural centers have temporary exhibits as well as permanent displays. The recently renovated Navy Pier is hosting many events, but at the time of publishing it's not known which will be annual events.

January

Skate on State
The Ice Skating Rink is open through March on State Street between Randolph and Washington streets. If you don't have your own skates you can rent them here, tel: 744-3370.

February

Chicago's Black History Month
Celebrated with good exhibitions and performances at museums and other cultural institutions.

Azalea Show
A gardeners' delight, at Garfield Park and Lincoln Park conservatories.

Chicago Auto Show
New cars are unveiled at McCormick Place, tel: 791-7000.

March

Medinah Shrine Circus
Held at Medinah Temple 600 N. Wabash Avenue tel: 266-5000.

St. Patrick's Day Parade
This is the biggest and oldest of the downtown parades; it follows Dearborn Street from Wacker Drive to Van Buren Street. The Chicago River is even dyed bright green every year to

Chicago blooms

celebrate the day, tel: 942-9188.

South Side Irish Parade
A family oriented parade that is held on the Sunday before St. Patrick's Day. It starts at 103rd Street going South on Western Avenue in the Beverly neighborhood, tel: 773-239-7755.

April

Spring Flower Show
Catch it at Garfield Park and Lincoln Park conservatories.

May

Buckingham Fountain
The fountain reopens in Grant Park, featuring nightly colored lights.

June

Chicago Blues Festival
Petrillo Band Shell in Grant Park, tel: 744-3370. Early June.

Chicago Gospel Festival
Petrillo Band Shell in Grant Park, tel: 744-3370. Mid-June.

Chicago Country Music Festival
Petrillo Band Shell in Grant Park, tel: 744-3370. Late June.

Old Town Art Fair
1900 N. Lincoln Avenue, tel: 337-1938.

Taste of Chicago
Held in Grant Park and featuring food from a large variety of Chicago restaurants, plus plenty of music and entertainment, tel: 744-3370. Last week of June and beginning of July.

Ravinia
The setting for a summer of outdoor concerts in Highland Park. Sit in the pavilion or picnic in the grass.

Grant Park Concerts
Offered free at Petrillo Band Shell in Grant Park by the Grant Park Symphony Orchestra, tel: 744-3370.

July

Taste of Chicago
The Fest continues, culminating in a spectacular fireworks display over Lake Michigan, accompanied by the Grant Park Symphony Orchestra performing Tchaikovsky's *1812 Overture*.

Fourth of July
A celebration with fireworks on the lakefront and throughout Chicago.

Taste of Lincoln Avenue
Lincoln Park's food fair at Fullerton and Wrightwood, tel: 773-880-5200.

World's Largest Block Party
Join it at Old St. Patrick's Church, Adams and Des Plaines streets, tel: 782-6171.

Chicago to Mackinac Yacht Races
Sail from Monroe Street Harbor, tel: 861-7777.

Venetian Night
Evening boat parade from Monroe Harbor to the Shedd Aquarium, tel: 744-3370.

August

Chicago Air and Water Show
North Avenue Beach, tel: 744-3370. Late August.

Chicago Jazz Festival
Petrillo Band Shell in Grant Park, tel: 744-3370. Late August.

Illinois State Fair
Held every year in Springfield, the capital of Illinois.

September

Viva Chicago
Latin Music Festival at Petrillo Band Shell in Grant Park, tel: 744-3370.

Mid September.
Oktoberfest
Celebrated at the Berghoff Restaurant and other Chicago pubs, tel: 427-3170.

October

Columbus Day Parade
Follow it on Dearborn Street from Wacker Drive to Congress Street.
The Chicago Marathon
A 26.2 mile run in Grant Park. Also a 3.1 mile run and a wheelchair run.
The Chicago International Film Festival
A presentation of new American and foreign films to the city.

November

Skate on State
Open after Thanksgiving, weather permitting, tel: 744-3370.
Christmas Around the World
A display of Christmas trees decorated in the traditional style of various countries held at the Museum of Science and Industry.
Chrysanthemum Show
Held at Lincoln Park and Garfield Park conservatories.

Chicago Film Festival

The Magnificent Mile Light Festival
The holiday season is kicked off with a myriad of tiny white lights on Michigan Avenue, tel: 642-3570.
Lighting of the City's Christmas Tree
Held the day after Thanksgiving, in Daley Center Plaza, tel: 744-3370.
Christmas Parade
Catch it on Michigan Avenue the Saturday after Thanksgiving. Santa is scheduled to be there.

December

Caroling to the Animals
At Lincoln Park Zoo, tel: 742-2000.
A Christmas Carol
Performed at the Goodman Theater, tel: 443-3800.
The Nutcracker
Performed at Arie Crown Theater at McCormick Place, tel: 902-1500.

Oktoberfest at the Berghoff Restaurant

Practical Information

GETTING THERE

By Air

Chicago is served by two major airports. Chicago O'Hare International Airport is located about 18 miles from downtown on the Kennedy Expressway (I 90/94) at Mannheim Road and has an international terminal and three domestic terminals. Information booths are situated on the lower level of each terminal, while the upper level of the international terminal also has an information booth and a foreign currency exchange. Tel: 686-2200 for general airport information.

High expectations

The cheapest way to get to downtown from the airport is with the Chicago Transit Authority (the CTA), which is very inexpensive and takes about 45 minutes. Trains leave from inside the terminal on the lower level every 5 to 10 minutes, except between 1am and 5am when they run every 30 minutes. Continental Airport Express provides a van service between O'Hare and all major downtown hotels for around $15 one way or around $25 round trip. Vans depart every 5 minutes, tel: 454-7799. Taxis are available on the lower level of each terminal from 6am to 1am, and cost between $25 and $30. the Shared-Ride program charges a cheaper flat rate. Car rentals or limousine services can be arranged at booths near the baggage claim area.

Midway Airport, 5700 S. Cicero, is about 7 miles southwest of downtown Chicago. The one building is divided into three terminals in this altogether smaller, less crowded alternative for domestic flights, tel: 454-7800.

The cheapest way to get downtown from Midway is also by the CTA. Trains leave from a station connected to the east side of the airport, and run Monday to Saturday 5am–11:30pm, and on Sunday and holidays from 7.30am–11.30pm. Continental Airport Express is located across from the Southwest Airlines ticket counter. Vans departing for downtown leave every 15-20 minutes, and charge around $10 one-way or around $20 round trip. Taxis are located in front of the main terminal; the 20-30 minute ride costs between $20 and $25. The Shared-Ride program charges a flat rate of around $10. Car rentals or limousine services can be arranged near the baggage claim area.

The El – a Chicago mover 'n' shaker

By Bus

Greyhound/Trailways has nationwide service to its main terminal downtown at Clark and Randolph streets.

It also has two neighborhood stations: the 95th Street and Dan Ryan Expressway CTA station on the southwest side and the Cumberland CTA station at 5800 N. Cumberland Avenue on the northwest side near O'Hare Airport. Tel: 781-2900 to obtain fare and schedule information.

By Rail

Amtrak offers passenger rail service from Union Station at Jackson and Canal Streets. Tel: 1-800-USA-RAIL (872 7245) for Amtrak information.

By Road

The major east-west route across northern Illinois is I-80, which passes near Chicago from Indiana to the east or Iowa to the west.

Coming from the north, the main interstates, I-90 and I-94, merge about 10 miles north of downtown to form the Kennedy Expressway (I-90/94), a direct route to downtown.

I-57 runs through Illinois from the south, and connects with the Dan Ryan Expressway (I-90/94) to reach the downtown area. You'll notice that I-90/94 is referred to by two different names: the Kennedy north of downtown, and the Dan Ryan to the south.

TRAVEL ESSENTIALS

Visas and Passports

To enter the United States, travelers must have a valid passport. Before departing from their own countries, foreign visitors should contact the nearest United States Embassy or Consulate to find out if a visa is necessary.

Weather

Chicago is a great place to experience all four seasons. Summers get pretty hot and humid, but due to breezes off Lake Michigan, it's usually as much as 10 degrees cooler near the lake. Winter in Chicago means cold temperatures, often with snow. Spring brings its share of rain, but temperatures are moderate, as they are in autumn. A common saying in Chicago is 'If you don't like the weather, wait an hour, it'll change'. For an up-to-date weather forecast, call 967-1212.

Average Daily High Temperatures (Fahrenheit)	
January	29
February	34
March	44
April	59
May	70
June	79
July	85
August	82
September	76
October	64
November	48
December	35

Clothing

Dress for the season. Winter weather requires a very warm coat, hat, gloves, and, in case of snow, a pair of boots. In summer, dress for hot, humid weather and bring a swimsuit to enjoy the beaches along Lake Michigan. It cools off quite a bit at night, especially near the lake, and almost all buildings are air conditioned, so bring along a light jacket or sweater too. Casual wear is acceptable in most places, but if you're planning to visit posh, swanky night-

Dressing for the season

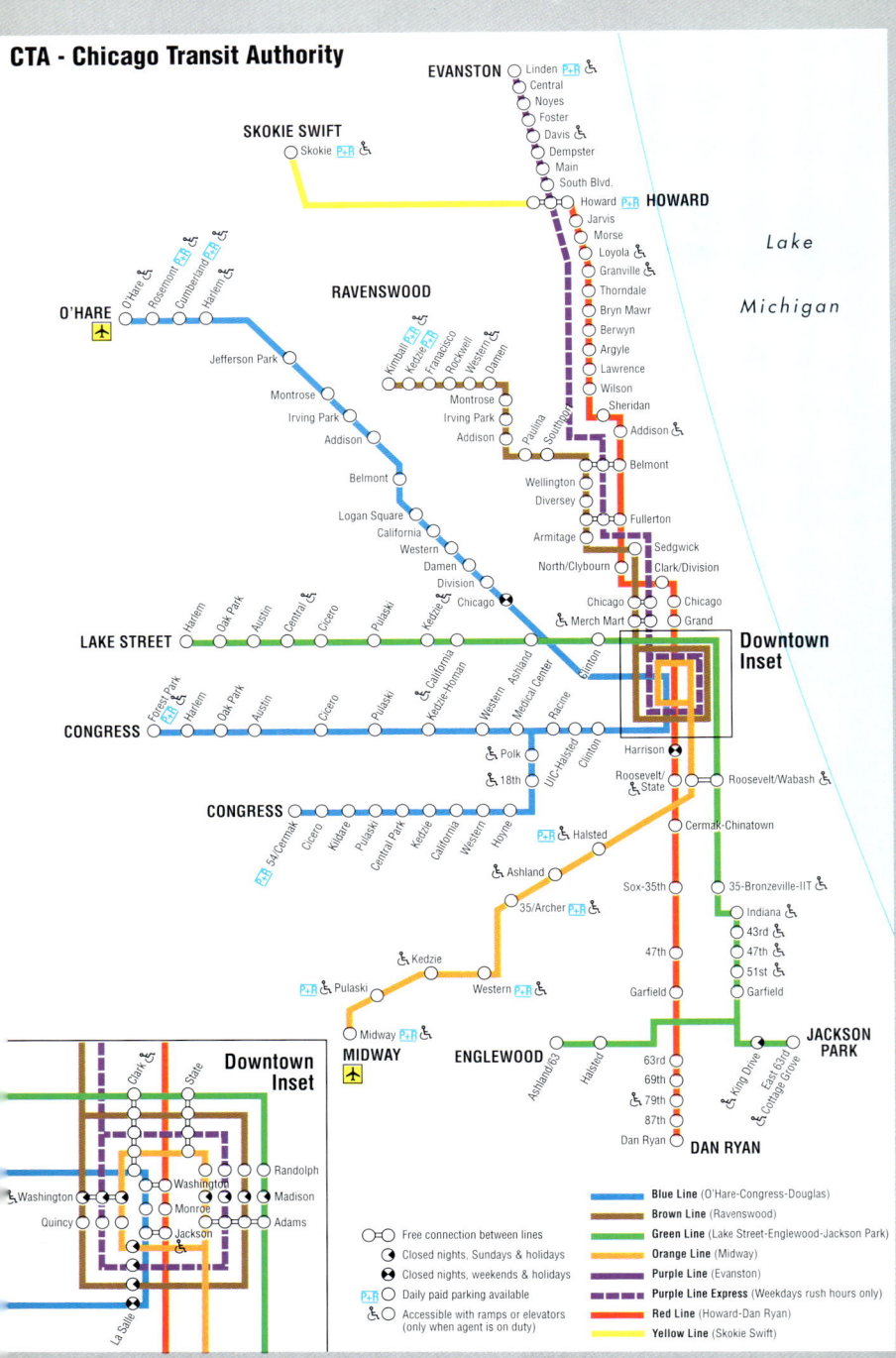

clubs, restaurants or the theater, take something a little more formal (jacket and tie for men, dress or pants suit for women).

Electricity

The standard is 110 volts. European appliances will require an adapter to connect plug to outlet and a converter to adjust the voltage.

GETTING ACQUAINTED

Government and Economy

Chicago isn't just a political town, it's a Democratic town in a Republican state, with the Democrats carrying a great deal of power in the state. Richard M Daley, whose father Richard J Daley was mayor for 21 years from 1955 to 1976, is the current mayor of the city, since his election in 1989. Jesse Jackson, Sr and Jr, both had their start in Chicago. Chicago has a city council form of government, with mayor as head honcho of the council. The city is divided into wards, based on population, and each ward elects an alderman to represent them on the council. In theory, this is a strong council/weak mayor system. In reality, the mayor of Chicago wields a great deal of power.

Chicago's economy is based on big business. A great deal of Chicago's business involves retail sales, and as service is important for retaining customers you can expect prompt attention and courtesy in the stores.

Geography

Chicago is located in the northeast corner of Illinois at the southwest tip of Lake Michigan, which constitutes the city's entire eastern border; the city's other large waterway is the Chicago River. Although Chicago is by far the best-known city in Illinois, the state capital is actually Springfield, located 200 miles to the south.

It's an easy city to navigate as it's laid out in a grid pattern: the State and Madison intersection is the center point and all addresses are north, south, east, or west of that point. Each block is equal to 100 address numbers so, for example, 800 North State Street is eight blocks north of Madison. Keep in mind that Lake Michigan is to the east and you won't go very far wrong.

The lakefront, intended for recreational use, consists of beaches, parks, and gardens. West of the lakefront is the downtown area of businesses, stores, and hotels which make up Chicago's famous skyline. Encircling the downtown area are diverse residential neighborhoods. Surrounding Chicago in an ever-widening band are the suburbs, which often, but not always, follow the address numbering pattern used in the city.

Population

Chicago is often called a city of neighborhoods. The city, current population 3 million, grew at a tremendous rate following the Chicago Fire, and ethnic enclaves developed. Often the place to find a particular type of restaurant is in the corresponding neighborhood.

GETTING AROUND

Taxis

Taxi cabs are plentiful. Just step off the curb and raise your arm. Rates are around $1.50 plus a few cents extra for each additional 1/6 of a mile and extra for 45 seconds of waiting time. There's a small surcharge for each additional passenger between the ages of 12 and 65. A 15 per cent tip is standard for the driver. A cab between O'Hare Airport and Chicago costs $25-$30. From Midway Airport to

Along for the ride

downtown costs $20-$25. If you need to order a cab to come and pick you up, call one of these companies: Checker Taxi, tel: 243-2537, or Yellow Cab Company, tel: 829-4222.

Public Transportation

Chicago's bus and rail system is operated by the Chicago Transit Authority (CTA). Bus stops are marked with signs indicating the bus routes they serve. There are seven train lines, commonly called the El (short for elevated), indicated by color. The rate for both trains and buses is the same, with a transfer available for an extra charge. The transfer must be requested on your first ride, and is good for two more rides in a two-hour time period. You can also buy a CTA card which does the same job more efficiently. There is a cheaper children's rate, and children under seven ride free. Note that bus drivers require exact change. Call the CTA, tel: 836-7000, for information on which train or bus will get you to your destination. Simply tell them where you are and where you want to go.

Cars

Plates to go

If you're concentrating on the downtown area, you can get along nicely without a car, in fact having one can be a liability, especially when trying to park. Public transportation and a little walking will get you to all the places we discuss.

If you do have a car, check with your hotel to see if parking is included in your room rate or available through the hotel. On-street parking is difficult to find, and usually time restricted. And while there are plenty of parking lots, using these several times a day can be ruinously expensive as well as time-consuming. For the undeterred here is a list of the major car rental firms:

Alamo Rent A Car   800-327-9403
Avis Rent A Car   800-331-1212
Budget Rent A Car   800-527-0700
Dollar Rent A Car   800-800-4000
Enterprise Rent A Car   800-325-8007
Hertz Rent A Car   800-654-3131

HOURS AND HOLIDAYS

Business Hours

Businesses and government offices are generally open 9am–5pm, Monday through Friday. Due to the large number of commuters the hour before 9am and after 5pm are the busiest times on the roads. If possible avoid driving during these times.

Public Holidays

New Year's Day: January 1
Martin Luther King's birthday: January 15
President's Day: 3rd Monday in February
Memorial Day: Last Monday in May
Independence Day: July 4
Labor Day: 1st Monday in September
Columbus Day: 2nd Monday in October
Veterans' Day: November 11
Thanksgiving: 4th Thursday in November
Christmas: December 25

ACCOMMODATION

Since most of the activities suggested in this book are in and around downtown, the hotels recommended here are all in the general downtown area. Three (see South Loop) are south of the river near theaters, some museums and the McCormick Place convention center.

Hotels in big cities are generally expensive, and unfortunately Chicago is no exception. You may pay a premium price, but you'll get a lot for your money, from the ambiance of your room to an elaborate lobby and first-rate service. Some of the less expensive hotels don't offer fancy rooms and amenities are scarce, but you can't beat the location for the price. Inquire about special rates – deals such as weekend rates are often offered.

Prices apply to a standard double room for one night. Prices have been categorized as follows: **$** = under $100; **$$** = $100-$150; **$$$** = $150-$200; **$$$$** = $200-$250; **$$$$$** = over $250.

Hotel Inter-Continental

DAYS INN *(578 rooms)*
644 North Lake Shore Drive 60611
Tel: 943-9200/ 1-800-325-2525
Fax: 649-5580
No frills, but great location for the price. Near North Pier, and just two blocks to a beach. $$

THE DRAKE *(535 rooms)*
140 E. Walton Place, 60611
Tel: 787-2200/ 1-800-553-7253
Fax: 787-6324
The city's most famous hotel opened in 1920, and has been the choice of heads of state ever since. Built on North Michigan Avenue to resemble an Italian Renaissance palace, the Drake is in the National Register of Historic Places.

The oak-paneled lobby has a marble fountain and high tea is served in the plush, lush Palm Court. Rooms resemble those in an English country house; each is a little different, but all have sitting areas and ample space. Expect service. Restaurant: Cape Cod Room. Oak St. Beach is just across the street. Check out the bar Le Coq D'Or for piano music. $$$$

EMBASSY SUITES *(358 suites)*
600 North State Street, 60610
Tel: 943-3800/ 1-800-362-2779
Fax: 943-7629
All suites include a mini-kitchen and a sleeper sofa. Complimentary full breakfast. Fitness center, lap pool and laundry room available. $$$

FOUR SEASONS HOTEL *(343 rooms)*
120 East Delaware Place, 60611
Tel: 280-8800/ 1-800-332-3442
Fax: 280-9184
Visiting celebrities stay here for the pampering but the staff aims to treat every guest like a celebrity. You can expect excellent service.

Located above the 900 North Michigan Shops (Bloomingdale's) with the feel of an English country house, the lobby has a wood-burning fireplace and a marble fountain imported from Italy. Elegant afternoon tea is served daily. Ye Olde Worlde atmosphere is carried through to the guest rooms. $$$$$

HOTEL INTER-CONTINENTAL
(844 rooms)
505 North Michigan Avenue 60611
Tel: 944-4100/ 1-800-327-0200
Fax: 944-3050
Near the South end of the Magnificent Mile. It's actually two combined hotels, the original hotel built in 1929 and a more modern adjacent building; both recently renovated. $$$

MOTEL 6 *(190 rooms)*
162 East Ontario Street, 60611
Tel: 787-3580/ 1-800-621-8055
Fax: 787-2354
No frills, but great location and prices.

The Ritz Carlton

Just a block east of the Magnificent Mile. $

PARK HYATT *(255 rooms)*
800 North Michigan Avenue, 60611
Tel: 280-2222 / 1-800-233-1234
Fax: 649-2290
This small, elegant hotel attracts mostly corporate travelers during the week. Multilingual staff employed. At the time of writing the hotel is undergoing major renovation. $$$$

THE RAPHAEL HOTEL *(172 rooms)*
201 East Delaware Place, 60611
Tel: 943-5000 / 1-800-821-5343
Fax: 943-9483
This hotel, located just off Michigan Avenue near the John Hancock Center and Water Tower Place, has a distinct European atmosphere. It has a loyal following, attracting repeat customers. $$$

THE RITZ CARLTON *(430 rooms)*
160 East Pearson Street, 60611
Tel: 266-1000 / 1-800-621-6906
Fax: 266-1194

Since it's located above Water Tower Place, the two-story greenhouse lobby is actually on the twelfth floor. This ultra deluxe hotel has windows that open and spacious rooms. Afternoon tea and cocktails are served. $$$$$

THE FAIRMONT HOTEL *(692 rooms)*
200 North Columbus Drive, 60601
Tel: 565-8000 / 1-800-527-4727
Fax: 312-856-9020

Built in 1987 as part of the Illinois Center, the Fairmont overlooks Grant Park from the north. The spacious rooms feature extra long beds. Bathrooms have separate showers and oversize tubs, radio and TV. Windows can be opened to catch the lake breeze, a rare feature in high-rise hotels. The restaurant features operatic waiters. No health club, but discount to Illinois Center's superb facility, the Athletic Club. Metropole night club. $$$$

HYATT REGENCY *(2,019 rooms)*
151 East Wacker Drive, 60601
Tel: 565-1234 / 1-800-233-1234
Fax: 565-2966
This hotel is huge, has many meeting rooms, and is close to either State Street or Michigan Avenue shopping. Popular for business meetings. $$$$

SHERATON CHICAGO HOTEL AND TOWERS *(1,200 rooms)*
City Front Plaza
301 E. North Water Street, 60611
Tel: 464-1000 / 1-800-325-3535
Fax: 329-7045
With no neighboring skyscrapers, all rooms in this 34-story modern building have some type of view. Located one block east of Michigan Avenue adjacent to the Chicago River. Rooms are fairly small. There's a full health club, and the largest ballroom in the Midwest. $$$

STOUFFER RENAISSANCE HOTEL *(553 rooms)*
One West Wacker Drive
Tel: 372-7200 / 1-800-468-3571
Fax: 372-0093
This relatively new hotel is decorated with faux French Provincial furniture. Bellhops dress in traditional garb. Location is convenient to the Loop and Merchandise Mart. Most rooms have a good view. $$$$

SWISSOTEL *(630 rooms)*
323 East Wacker Drive, 60601
Tel: 565-0565 / 1-800-654-7263
Fax: 565-0540
Experience quiet European ambiance in this high rise building. Rooms include a sitting area. There's a health club and bakery selling home-baked goods. $$$

South Loop

BLACKSTONE HOTEL *(305 rooms)*
636 South Michigan Avenue, 60605
Tel: 427-4300 / 1-800-622-6320
Fax: 427-4736
Built in 1910, you can feel the history here. There are chandeliers and marble statues in the lobby. Every American President has stayed here since its opening. It

Hyatt Hotel

has large comfortable rooms with high ceilings. Home to the Mayfair Theatre where *Shear Madness* has been playing since 1982. $$

CHICAGO HILTON AND TOWERS
(1,543 rooms)
720 South Michigan, 60605
Tel: 922-4400/1-800-HILTONS
Fax: 922-5240
This vast convention hotel located across from Grant Park has the largest exhibition space, the largest health club, and the grandest ballroom of any in the city. Visit Kitty O'Shea's Irish Pub for live entertainment and to hear a real Irish brogue. $$$

THE PALMER HOUSE HILTON
(1,639 rooms)
17 East Monroe Street, 60603
Tel: 726-7500/1-800-445-8667
Fax: 263-2556
This 100-year-old landmark hotel in the Loop not far from the Art Institute has some of the most ornate and elegant public areas in the city. It features a street level shopping arcade with 25 shops. The main lobby is up one floor, with ceiling murals by Louis Rigal. Guest rooms have plenty of elbow room. $$$

COMMUNICATION AND NEWS

Telephone

The area code for downtown Chicago is 312. This does not need to be dialed if you are calling within the 312 area code. All the phone numbers in this book are in the 312 area code unless otherwise indicated. Areas outside downtown, but still in Chicago, require the use of the 773 area code, and the suburbs around Chicago have various area codes. If you're not sure which area code to use (and even Chicagoans are having trouble keeping them straight now that they keep adding new ones), simply dial 411 for Directory Assistance. Any calls to another area code must be preceded by the number 1.

Walkin' the talk

Newspapers

Chicago has two major daily newspapers, the *Chicago Tribune* and the *Chicago Sun-Times*. Both are morning papers carrying local, national and international news. Each has a section in their *Friday* edition with information on current entertainment events. The *Reader* is a free weekly paper distributed on Thursday, primarily on the north side, which also carries all the latest entertainment information. *Crain's* is a weekly paper for the latest

Street news

Family outing

Chicago business news. Many neighborhood, ethnic, and specialty publications are available. Some bookstores, such as Borders, carry foreign and out of town papers.

USEFUL INFORMATION

Children

Chicago Parent is a monthly publication highlighting events of interest to children and their families, as well as presenting articles of general interest about children. It's available free at locations throughout the city, including libraries and children's bookstores.

Many hotels let children stay in their parents' room for free. Restaurants frequently offer a special under-12 menu, with smaller portions and lower prices. Most museums and attractions offer discounted rates for children, and often let infants in for free.

Attractions

As much as possible was included in the itineraries, but some other attractions in the city include:

JANE ADDAMS HULL HOUSE
800 South Halsted Street
Tel: 413-5353
Founded by social worker Jane Addams, this former settlement house which served as a basis for inner-city social welfare programs is now a museum.

DUSABLE MUSEUM
740 East 56th Place
Tel: 773-947-0600
Dedicated to the collection, preservation and study of the history and culture of Africans and Americans of African descent.

MUSEUM OF HOLOGRAPHY
1134 West Washington Boulevard.
Tel: 226-1007

PEACE MUSEUM
314 West Institute Place
Tel: 440-1860
Art and history museum devoted to peace.

POLISH MUSEUM OF AMERICA
984 North Milwaukee Avenue
Tel: 773-384-3352

SPERTUS MUSEUM
618 South Michigan Avenue
Tel: 922-9012
Comprehensive collection of Judaic art and exhibits spanning 5,000 years of Jewish history and culture.

SWEDISH AMERICAN MUSEUM CENTRE
5211 North Clark Street
Tel: 773-728-8111

HAROLD WASHINGTON PUBLIC LIBRARY
400 South State Street
Tel: 747-4999
Chicago Public Library's main facility showcases a vast collection of over 2 million books. The library is named after Chicago's first black mayor.

Because there's so much to do in the city itself, I've concentrated on the downtown area. However, there are some attractions in the surrounding suburbs that are worth a trip:

BROOKFIELD ZOO
First Avenue and 31st Street, Brookfield
Tel: 708-242-2630
A bigger zoo than Lincoln Park. Tropic World features animals, including gorillas, in their natural habitat without walls between you and the animals. Porpoise Show in the Seven Seas Panorama is a

long-time favorite. Young children are enchanted by the Children's Petting Zoo. Daily 9.30am–6pm. Admission charge. Free Tuesday.

CHICAGO BOTANIC GARDEN
Lake Cook Road east of the Edens Expressway, Glenwood (25 miles north of Chicago)
Tel: 847-835-5440
Over 300 acres of gardens, lakes, trails, greenhouses, museum and restaurants.

SANTA'S VILLAGE
601 Dundee Avenue, Dundee
Tel: 847-426-6673
See Santa Claus every day at this amusement park. Young children especially seem to enjoy this, but there's also a waterpark next door, Racing Rapids, tel: 847-426-5525, that will please the older kids. May to September. Admission charge to both attractions.

SIX FLAGS GREAT AMERICA
I-94 at Grand Avenue, Gurnee
Tel: 847-249-1776
Large amusement park with over 130 rides, shows, and attractions, divided into seven themed areas. Emphasis on roller coasters. May to September. Admission charge.

USEFUL ADDRESSES

Emergency 911 Use this number for police, fire, or ambulance.
Time 976-1616
Weather 976-1212
Illinois Bureau of Tourism 800-223-0121 Will send a packet of information before your trip.
Mayor's Office of Special Events Hotline 744-3370
Chicago Office of Tourism 744-2400
Chicago Fine Arts Hotline 346-3278
Visitor Information Center (3 locations)
Chicago Cultural Center
77 East Randolph Street
Monday to Friday 10am–6pm, Saturday 10am–5pm, Sunday noon–5pm, closed holidays.
Historic Water Tower
806 N Michigan Avenue
Monday to Saturday 9.30am–7pm, Sunday 10am–6pm, closed holidays.
Illinois Market Place at Navy Pier
700 E Grand Avenue
Monday to Thursday 10am–9pm, Sunday 10am–7pm.

SPORTS

Chicago takes its sports almost as seriously as its politics; the city's major sports teams are covered in *Pick & Mix 9*. Horseracing is also an option, but if you have this in mind you'll have to go to the suburbs for it. Try Arlington International Racecourse, Euclid and Wilke

Cycling that cellulite

Beach bikers

Golf Illinois Center, 616-1234, is a par 3 nine-hole golf course and driving range east of Columbus Drive, south of the Chicago River. Club rentals are available. The Chicago Park District, tel: 294-2274, also offers a number of 9-hole courses, and one 18-hole course in Jackson Park, 63rd Street and Stony Island Drive.

In addition, many of the surrounding suburbs have courses open to the public. They'll be more expensive but they're generally more attractive courses.

In winter, ice skating is available at Daley Centennial Plaza; Skate on State; State Street between Washington and Randolph streets; or Navy Pier. Try tobogganing in the Cook County Forest Preserves, tel: 261-8400.

FURTHER READING

Boss: Richard J Daley of Chicago, Mike Royko, New York, 1971. The story of Mayor Richard J Daley.

Chicago Days: 150 Defining Moments in the Life of a Great City, by the staff of the *Chicago Tribune*, edited by Stevenson Swanson, Contemporary Books, 1997. Pictures and stories of defining events of Chicago.

Forever Open, Clear and Free: The Struggle for Chicago's Lakefront, Lois Wille, Chicago, 1991. Story of the fight to save Chicago's lakefront.

Insight Guide: Chicago, Martha Ellen Zenfell, editor, Apa Publications, 1996. Essays written by local experts, with a fact-packed information section.

Kids Explore Chicago, Susan D. Moffat, Adams Media Corp, 1995. Recommendations of activities children would enjoy in Chicago.

Navy Pier: A Chicago Landmark, by Douglas Bukowski, Metropolitan Pier and Exposition Authority, 1996. History of Navy Pier.

Streetwise Chicago: A History of Chicago Street Names, by Don Hayner and Tom McNamee, Loyola University Press, 1988. A fun look at Chicago through the history of its street names.

Sarah Paretsky's gritty crime novels, featuring tough, wise-cracking private eye V.I. Warshawski, are all set in Chicago.

streets, Arlington Heights, 847-670-3681.

If you'd like to participate in a sport, the Chicago Park District, tel: 294-2493 is a good source of information. The lake front is a great place to spend time, and there's much to do there. With 29 miles of beaches along the lakefront, there's always someplace to walk, run, bike, in-line skate, and of course swim. Beaches are open with lifeguards on duty in the summer months. Bikes or in-line skates can be rented for the day or hourly from Bike Chicago, 1-800-915-BIKE (2453), at Lincoln Park, Oak Street Beach, Navy Pier or Buckingham Fountain. They offer free bike maps and free delivery to your hotel for daily rentals.

Golfers, if not their spouses and partners, will be glad to know that their game is now available in the downtown area. Metro-

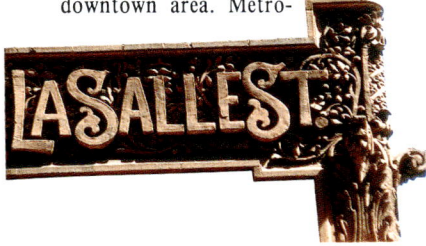

Index

A

Adler Planetarium 48, 50
Amoco Building 11
Andersonville 13
antiques 78
Antiques Etc A Mall 39
art galleries 64
Art Institute 20, 25
Austin Park 38–9
Avenue, The 38

B

baseball 13, 62–3
basketball 63
beaches 92
Beer Garden 33
Beverley 13
biking 92
Blackhawks 63
Blackstone Hotel 27
Block 37 52
Blue Chicago 59
Blue Chicago on Clark 59
B.L.U.E.S. 59
blues clubs 58-60
Blues Fest 58
bookstores 36, 57, 78
Bridgeport 13
Buckingham Fountain 25–6, 27
Buddy Guy's Legends 60
Burnham, Daniel H. 12, 17, 24
Byrne, Jane 17

C

Capone, Al 16–7, 60
Carson Pirie Scott 76
Cermak, Anton (Tony) 14, 17
Chicago Academy of Sciences 32
Chicago Architecture Foundation 45–6, 57
Chicago Bears 63
Chicago Blackhawks 63
Chicago Board of Trade 23
Chicago Bulls 63
Chicago Cubs 62
Chicago Cultural Center 52
Chicago Historical Society 44
Chicago O'Hare Airport 15, 17, 82
Chicago Place 30, 46
Chicago Stadium 32
Chicago Stock Exchange 25
Chicago Symphony Orchestra 27
Chicago Tribune 11
Chicago White Sox 62
children's activities 25, 31-4, 42-4, 48-50, 54-5, 60-1
Chinatown 13
churches
    Episcopal Cathedral of St James 31

Holy Name Cathedral 31
Medinah Temple 31
City Hall Cook County Building 51
City of Chicago Store 32
Cobb Hall 56
Comiskey Park 62
Conservatory, The 42
cruises 34
Crystal Gardens 33
CTA 20

D,E,F

Daley, Richard J. 14, 15, 17
Daley, Richard M. 15, 17
Dillinger, John 17
Dock Street 33
Du Sable, Jean Baptiste Point 10, 29
eating 68-71
ethnic groups and neighborhoods 13-4
events 79-81
Family Pavilion 33
FAO Schwartz 31, 46
Farm in the Zoo 44
Federal Center and Plaza 24
Field Museum 48-9
First National Bank Plaza 52
Flamingo 24
football 63
Fort Dearborn 10, 17, 28

G, H

Gallery 37 52
gangsters 16, 60-1
Ghirardelli Chocolate Shop and Soda Fountain 46
Ginko Tree Bookshop 37
Gold Coast Art Fair 65
Grand Ballroom 33
Grant Park 25-7
Grant Park Concert 26
Great Chicago Fire 10, 17, 28
Greektown 13
Hancock Observatory 34
Harpo Studios 66
Hemingway's Birthplace 38

Henry Crown Space Center 55
hockey 63
Holabird 11, 24, 51
Home and Studio 35-7
hotels 86-9
Hot Tix 21, 27, 30, 72
Hyde Park 13, 54

I,J,K

IMAX Theatre 33
Jahn, Helmut 12, 51
James R. Thompson Center 51
John G. Shedd Aquarium 48-9
John Hancock Center 11, 31, 34, 45-6
Jolliet, Louis 10, 24, 28
Jordan, Michael 17
King, Martin Luther 17
Kingston Mines 59

L,M

Lagoon, The 44
Lake Michigan 26
Lake Street 39
Lakeview 13
Lilly's 59
Lincoln Park 13, 42-4, 59
Lincoln Park Zoo 43
Loop, The 13, 21
Lord & Taylor 46
Magnificent Mile 13, 28-34, 45-7
Marquette Building 24
Marquette, Jacques 10, 24, 28
Marshall Field's 46, 76
McCormick Place 15
Medill, Joseph 11
Merchandise Mart 65
Michigan Avenue 13, 28-34, 45-7
Michigan Avenue Bridge 28
Midway Airport 82
Miro 51
Moore-Dugal Tour Home 37
Museums
    Chicago Children's Museum 33
    Hemingway Museum 38
    Museum of Broadcast

Communications 52
Museum of Contemporary Art 30
Museum of Science and Industry 54
Field Museum 49-50
Smart Museum 56
Terra Museum of American Art 30
music venues 58-60, 72-5

N, O

Navy Pier 15, 28, 32-4
NBC Tower 66
Neiman Marcus 46
Ness, Eliot 16
New Checkerboard Lounge 60
Nickerson Mansion 31
Nike Town 30, 47
900 North Michigan Shop 45
North Pier 32, 77
Oak Park 14, 20, 35-9
Oak Park Visitors Center 36
Oak Street 77
Oceanarium 49
Odyssey 34
O'Gara & Wilson Book Shop 57
Ogden, William B. 14, 17
Old Town 14, 44
O'Leary Mrs (and cow) 10
Orchestra Hall 27
Oriental Institute 56

P, Q

Palmer House 89
Petrillo Music Shell 25
Picasso Sculpture 17, 51
Powell's Bookstore 57
Pritzker Children's Zoo and Nursery 43
Prohibition 16, 24
Pumping Station 30

R

Renaissance Society 56
restaurants 68-71
    Avenue Cafe and Restaurant 47
    Berghoff Restaurant 24
    Cafe Brauer 44

Cafe Winberie 38
Carsons The Place for Ribs 65
Centro 65
Cheesecake Factory 45
Geppetto's 38
Grill, The 27
Hard Rock Cafe 61
Ice Cream Shoppe 44
Italian Village 26
L'Appetito Cafe 45
Lino's 65
Lou Mitchell's 22
Mac Kelly's Deli 51
Michael Jordan's Restaurant 61
Miller's Pub 26
Mitchell's Lou 21
Nick's Fishmarket 26
O'Brien's Restaurant & Bar 44
Petersen's 37
Philanders of Oak Park 39
Piccolo Mondo 56
Pizzeria Uno 31
Pizzeria Due 32
Prairie 27
Riva 34
Robie House 56
Rock-N-Roll McDonald's 61
Signature Room at the 95th 34
Tommy Gun's Restaurant 61
Un Grand Cafe 44
Richard J. Daley Center 50-2
River North 64
Robie House 56
Rockefeller Memorial Chapel 56
Rohe, Mies van der 11
Rookery 23–4
Roosevelt, Franklin D. 14
Root, John 24

S

Saks Fifth Avenue 46
Sandburg, Carl 17
Sears Tower 11, 17, 22–3
Sears Tower Skydeck 22
Second City 44

Second City E.T.C 44
shopping 45-7, 76-8
Skate on State 52
Sky Theater 50
Soldier Field 63
South Pond 43
Spirit of Chicago 34
Stockyards 10, 13, 17
St Valentine's Day Massacre 16
SuHu 64
Sullivan, Louis 11

T

Taste of Chicago 25, 68
taxis 85
theaters 73
   Goodman 27
   Mayfair 27
   Oak Park Festival Theater 39
   Omnimax 55
   Schubert 27
   Victory Gardens Theater 44
Tribune Building / Tower 12, 29
Tribune Store 47

University of Chicago 17, 55
Untouchables, The 16
Untouchables Tour 60
Viacom Entertainment Center 29–30
Village Players 39
Visitors Center 30
Ward, Montgomery 12
Washington, Harold 17
Water Tower 28, 30
Water Tower Place 31, 46
Winfrey, Oprah 65–6
Wright, Frank Lloyd 11, 14, 17, 24, 35-8
Wrigley Building 29
Wrigley Field 13, 62, 63
Zanies Comedy Club 44

U, V, W, Z

Union Station 22
United Center 63
Unity Temple 35-8

ACKNOWLEDGMENTS

Photography   Glyn Genin *and 8/9* Image Bank
Production Editor   Mohammed Dar
Handwriting   V Barl
Cover Design   Klaus Geisler
Cartography   Berndtson & Berndtson